MANDENTITY

Healing the Wounded Man

ADAM FRENCH

Room4God Publications
Nashville, Tennessee

MANdentity

Copyright © 2021 by Adam French

Published by Room4God Publications
adamfrench294@gmail.com
theadamfrench.com

Library of Congress Control Number: 2021912123

ISBN: 978-1-7369334-5-9

Printed in the United States of America

CONTENTS

ACKNOWLEDGMENTS 4

INTRODUCTION: LEARNING TO LOVE 6

ACCEPTING YOUR REALITY 16

FINDING THE POWER 33

SURRENDER TO WIN 47

GETTING HONEST 63

FINDING THE PAIN 79

CONFESSION 83

DISCOVERING HOW TO FEEL 98

IDENTIFYING OUR CHARACTER 117

PRACTICING FORGIVENESS 138

HEART CHECK 153

MEETING WITH JESUS 180

HELPING OTHERS 195

About the Author 211

ACKNOWLEDGMENTS

This book is a reflection of those who have chosen to love, support and encourage me in spite of my wounds. I want to thank my wife Josie for believing in me when I didn't believe in myself. As well as my two sons, J. R. and Joseph, for fueling the desire to change my life. And to my precious Stella for softening my heart in such a way that the words of this book could come.

I also want to thank my dad, Bob French Jr., my mother, Penny and my brother, Justin. They've known me at my worst and at my best, but their love never changed. This book in some ways in not a fair representation of them, as it mainly highlights our painful moments together. This is intentional so that men across the world can relate to my wounds and I pray my story helps heal their wounds. I want to clearly state that my father, mother, and brother are wonderful people and have taught me many things. I am grateful for the family that I have.

I also want to thank Men of Valor for presenting a need and equipping me to meet it with this book. There have been countless men and women that have invested in my life and helped me find the healing necessary to complete this book. I most certainly could not name them all. Their wisdom, grace and genuine desire shaped me into a MANdentity man, and for that I am eternally grateful.

Because of them and my willingness to follow the principles of this book, God has transformed my life. It has given me the opportunity to help men all across the world. If you feel led to have me come speak or share my story at a pulpit, classroom, conference, retreat, school assembly, business or youth camp go to theadamfrench.com or @theadamfrench for bookings.

I pray that everyone who reads the words and answers the questions in the next twelve chapters will find healing and learn tools to continue healing. God, please bless the person reading this book!

INTRODUCTION: LEARNING TO LOVE

A warm sensation started at the back of my neck and traveled its way throughout my body. *What is that?* I thought, becoming anxious. It was Christmas Eve and everyone was lounging on the massive sectional watching Chevy Chase try to find the bad bulb. No one had any idea what I was experiencing. It was similar to the rush felt just before speaking in front of a large crowd or before an important event except this sensation wasn't fleeting; it lingered throughout my body. Prior to this I had absolutely no indications of anything being wrong. The ministry that I pastored was transforming lives. People were experiencing God and there was genuine community centered around Scripture. Just a few weeks earlier the church had personally taken me to a leadership guru and infused me with confidence. They encouraged me with all that God had accomplish thus far through the ministry I shepherded. My life was good and was headed in the right direction, or at least I thought it was.

After seeing a doctor about the warm sensations and an extreme adverse reaction to the medication prescribed, I lay in our study on a twin bed that my wife had placed on the floor. She didn't

6

want our children to see me in the state I was in. It was three o'clock on a Sunday morning. I was fluctuating between intense warm sensations to cold sweaty shivers; it had been four days since I'd slept. From exercising three days a week and leading at a high capacity, I was now hanging on by a thread in a dark hole of uncertainty. Clinching my prayer cards and Scripture cards while mumbling prayers throughout the night, I was at a rock bottom like I had never experienced.

As the sun rose and a little light began to peak through the windows and illuminate all the books about God I had studied, the most important question I have ever asked came to me: How did I get here? This sent me on a journey for healing that led me to write this book.

It turns out I was experiencing anxiety, triggered by childhood trauma. My head, my body, my spirit were disconnected from each other. I consciously disassociated the chronic fear and abandonment that flow in a river deep beneath the surface of my emotions. I had to as a survival tactic. Deep wounds from my past now spewed out in anxiety from the slightest triggers. My body was saying the same thing it said when I was a child and a teen, "I don't feel safe." Now, I was listening. My connection with God was more religious than personal. I was full of all kinds of head knowledge gained through books, the Bible, conferences, seminars, sermons, and the list goes on. I was morally healthy, intellectually strong, driven as a leader, and doing the right things for my family and friends, but I was emotionally disconnected, spiritually out of rhythm, and out of touch with my inner self. Lost in formality and distant from the *me* deep inside. In short, I was a pastoral robot programmed to love and lead but incapable of *deep* soul-touching human and heavenly connection. I could feel on the surface, but beneath the surface my soul was numb like an iceberg floating in the artic with only a mile or two of its surface visible to the eye, while ten miles of mass floats deep beneath. So much of my pain and trauma, so much of my past, so much of my struggles that I did not understand.

My wife had noticed my inability to have emotional intimacy in our relationship for years. We had multiple conversations about it, but my response was to try harder and not dig deeper. It was as if what I had read and learned didn't touch my soul. I understood but didn't understand me, so the connection between understanding God and myself was severed. My consciousness was unable to correspond with my soul. How can you be out of touch with your inner self?

There are actually many ways this can happen with both men and woman, and more often it happens to men, which is who I'm speaking to in this book. This type of disconnect is often the cornerstone of behaviors such as drug use, adultery, narcissism, alcoholism, rage, rebellion, co-dependence, sexual addiction, anxiety and/or depression, workaholism, or unhealthy emotional reasoning. Many disconnected men wonder why they can't love and connect with their families well. Others have given up on their ability to connect and love more deeply. I'm not sure how or what brought you to pick up this book, but it is for a purpose. If you have just a tiny bit of willingness, this book has the capability of healing places within you that you did not even know were there. It can provide the tools to experience your life, and the people in it, more richly than ever before.

It will provide a foundation for continuous healing and growing and loving more deeply as the days, weeks, months, and years pass by. I can promise you this, you will be a better man because of it. It is time for you to discover an emotional and spiritually healing like never before.

HOW DOES THIS WORK?

MANdentity men receive the love that is extended to them.
1 John 4:19 "We love because he first loved us."

Wounded men have so much to tell and so much to learn. It is my desire to help broken men connect with a part of themselves they did not know existed, much less knew was broken. How does a man embark on a journey to heal something that he doesn't know is broken? How does a man set off on an expedition to find something when he is uncertain of where it is? As men, we journey to distance places and take up causes that require us to face extreme challenges, but rarely do we attempt these things without any training. As men we want to be prepared. Let me prepare you for the content in this book.

Every man is wounded in some way and unhealed wounds become struggles. They become spiritual, emotional, and physical strongholds that cause wounds from which one desires to break free. So how do you break free and begin healing? In this book I help you identify the struggles causing broken connections deep in your soul. This is not just a read, circle, underline, and highlight type of book. It requires work, something men were created for. Man was placed in the garden to work before sin entered our world. A balanced work life is not a sin. Genesis 2:15 "The LORD God took the man and put him in the Garden of Eden to work it and take care of it." Think of your work in this book as a soul-care mission.

This is the most important work you will ever do. Your soul matters. It will become the foundation from which everything else in your life is built. Healing emotionally and spiritually is powerful, transformative and often the missing piece to healing the wounded man. When done honestly and without reservation it opens us up to the most powerful things in life: self-awareness, peace, hope, contentment, healthy relationships and much more.

This book is not about getting you to conform to a set of rules or outward disciplines, although you will grow significantly in spiritual disciplines. Instead, this book will help you discover who you are based on what you've done, what's been done to you, and who Scripture says you are. It's about helping you connect with your soul and with God. This book helps make you whole, giving you a strong foundation on which the rest of your life will be framed. It's a book designed to perform spiritual heart surgery.

I must warn you though. While this journey is simple, it is not easy. It will require effort on your part. When working through the questions in each chapter, you will need to find a quiet place, set aside ample time, say a prayer, and find a trusted mentor to support you. If you work this book honestly and hold nothing back, you can have emotional consistency, healthier relationships, spiritual balance, freedom from addictions and find healing for the broken connections in your life. You will realize a centeredness that will drastically improve your quality of life and most importantly teach you how to have a *real* relationship with Jesus while discovering the *real* you. This is a guide to healing the wounded man and a practical journey to unleashing his true MANdentity!

You will notice abrupt starts and stops to the stories I share in this book. These breaks are for you to pause, pray, and think about any similarities in your own story. Allow God to speak through the vulnerable pieces of my story to prepare you for the task of inspecting the emotional story beneath the surface of your own life. Do not leave any question unanswered, as it might be the one piece needed to make you completely whole.

This book can be completed by one man sharing with a trusted friend, or it can be worked through with a small group of men that meets and shares the answers to their questions out loud. Ideally, each man would complete one chapter a week. My heart is that whether done in a group or one on one, each man will answer each question with complete honesty to the best of his ability. Anything less will hinder the healing of the wounded man. I strongly suggest that this book not be worked through alone. At the minimum commit to sharing the answers to the questions with someone.

Finally, this book is not an end, but rather a beginning. I encourage you to go through this book over and over again. Once you've completed the book, consider leading a group of men in your circle through this book. It can only help them and you. You will be doing a service to the kingdom of God as you help men recognize their MANdentity.

MANdentity Truths

MANdentity Truths are an anchor for your soul, and the guardrails that lead you toward the light of Christ. In the beginning the light may seem distant and dim, but as you work through this book the light will get brighter. I think of MANdentity truths as our flashlight and like the little boy who was given a flashlight by his mother said, "Let's go find some darkness!" The light or MANdentity truths will gradually expose more of your struggles and your strengths. Be encouraged because these truths and Scripture references will help you grow and thrive along the way. My prayer is that these MANdentity Truths will be principles that serve as both an anchor for your soul and as guardrails for your daily life. Meditate on them often.

MANdentity men accept responsibility. (CHAPTER 1)

"Whoever conceals his transgressions will not prosper, but he who confesses and forsakes them will obtain mercy." (Proverbs 28:13 ESV)

MANdentity men rely on God's strength above their own. (CHAPTER 2)

"Trust in the LORD forever, for the LORD GOD is an everlasting rock." (Isaiah 26:4 ESV)

MANdentity men surrender their will over to Christ's will. (CHAPTER 3)

"I have been crucified with Christ and I no longer live, but Christ lives in me. The life I now live in the body, I live by faith in the Son of God, who loved me and gave himself for me." (Galatians 2:20)

MANdentity men are honest with themselves, others, and God. (CHAPTER 4)

"Having put away falsehood, let each one of you speak the truth with his neighbor, for we are members one of another." (Ephesians 4:25 ESV)

MANdentity men reject passivity. (CHAPTER 5)

"Do not merely listen to the word, and so deceive yourselves. Do what it says." (James 1:22)

MANdentity men regularly confess sin. (CHAPTER 6)

"Therefore confess your sins to each other and pray for each other so that you may be healed. The prayer of a righteous person is powerful and effective." (James 5:16)

MANdentity men express how they feel in a healthy way. (CHAPTER 7)

"And after you have suffered a little while, the God of all grace, who has called you to his eternal glory in Christ, will himself restore, confirm, strengthen, and establish you." (1 Peter 5:10 ESV)

MANdentity men pursue Godly character. (CHAPTER 8)

"When I was a child, I spoke like a child, I thought like a child, I reasoned like a child. When I became a man, I gave up childish ways." (1 Corinthians 13:11 ESV)

MANdentity men ask for forgiveness and offer forgiveness. (CHAPTER 9)

"For if you forgive others their trespasses, your heavenly Father will also forgive you, but if you do not forgive others their trespasses, neither will your Father forgive your trespasses."
(Matthew 6:14-15 ESV)

MANdentity men establish consistent accountability in their lives. (CHAPTER 10)

"Where no counsel is, the people fall: but in the multitude of counsellors there is safety." (Proverbs 11:14 BRG)

MANdentity men connect with Jesus through prayer, Bible reading, and Scripture memory. (CHAPTER 11)

"Jesus said to him, "I am the way, and the truth, and the life. No one comes to the Father except through me." (John 14:6)

MANdentity men serve their family, their church, and their community. (CHAPTER 12)

"For you were called to freedom, brothers. Only do not use your freedom as an opportunity for the flesh, but through love serve one another. For the whole law is fulfilled in one word: 'You shall love your neighbor as yourself.'"
(Galatians 5:13-14 ESV)

1
ACCEPTING YOUR REALITY

Sliding open the window of my room my friend and I were about to jump out, but I hesitated when I heard my brother crying in the other room. Dad slammed his truck door and headed toward the house with rifle in hand. "Bob, no. Bob, stop!" my mother shouted from outside. My friend jumped out the window, but I stood frozen by the door. It wasn't a moment of courage as much as a moment of resolve.

Putting my finger on how we came to that moment is difficult. Dad was always distant and pretty occupied with himself, but he was rarely violent except when giving us boys a good whooping. When Dad's construction business began to grow so did the pressure. Once as a kid while driving and drinking a beer, as he normally did, he told me he had a lot of equipment debt and needed to make several thousand dollars just to break even each month. My blank stare caused him to quickly move on. He realized I was clueless about bills, pressure, and anxiety of that sort. Besides we never really talked about anything meaningful. He drove and I rode. I worked and he gave orders. I disobeyed and he corrected me. That was about the gist of our conversations apart from the occasionally hunting lesson.

Around that time Dad began staying out at night. We started eating dinner without him and watching television without him. He started to miss my sporting events. Sometimes he would come home really late, and he'd be dirty and drunk. He didn't really say much. He'd take a quick shower and then pass out on the couch before being moved to the bed by my mom. I guess he decided that drinking himself into oblivion was the best way to cope with his struggles. After a while mom started waking us up and driving thirty minutes to the bar to fetch him. I remember one time piling in the minivan and being wide awake as we drove to get my dad. My brother snored next to me as I watched my mom's eyes in the review mirror. I could tell she was broken, scared, but I noticed an intense resolve deep inside. She wasn't giving up.

The back tires skidded in the rocky parking lot as my mom hit the brakes and flung open the door. She went in and then came back a few minutes later breathing hard and crying. She turned and looked at me and said, "come inside with me." Can you visualize this? A five-foot blonde-haired mom in her early thirties stomping into the bar with her thirteen-year-old son. Hoping to guilt her husband into leaving. My dad and I locked eyes, and she told me to go back to the van. The next thing I know the sliding back passenger door flew open as my dad fell to the ground mumbling incoherently.

I helped pull him all the way inside, and he yelled, "woman" a few times before drifting into a drunken snore.

Over the next few years, I was awakened many nights. Dad had started drinking more heavily at home, and he had become angry. He would try to rough up my mom. She tried to defend herself the best she could. One night she woke me up looking in my closet for a metal bat to defend herself. Then one day everyone disappeared. My mom and dad began staying at a camper by the lake, which was really close to where my dad's shop was, and my brother went to college. When he left he was studious and trustworthy, an anchor for our family. When he came back he was a partying addict that could not be counted on. I was alone most of the time. At first I loved the freedom. I was sixteen with a car, a fridge full of beer, and a house to myself. As the days turned to weeks and then months and then years, things got worse. My mom eventually came back alone from that little camper, and my dad and brother never returned. She was depressed and addicted to pills now. My freedom turned to loneliness and fear, and my self-worth slowly declined.

So anyway, my friend had jumped out the window and there I was standing by the door wondering if Dad would come down the hallway to try and shoot my brother and I. I thought him being missing for three days was normal, but it should have been a warning to me of what was to come. He wanted to kill us because he tried to rough up Mom again, and my brother stepped in. Dad attacked him, and I came in hitting him repeatedly with a hard pole, injuring the right side of his face. Once he let go of my brother he ran to the truck for the gun. Thankfully he sat down in the chair that night and said nothing before passing out into his drunken snore. Our family never woke up from that one. After it was all over, we never discussed the incident; we just moved on like nothing happened.

Thankfully, my athletics gave me plenty of opportunities to be away from home and provided fillers for the loneliness. Being athletic was a gift from God, and it gave me a safe place to be. I was one of the few white kids in the backfield of our freshman football team. Although I had never been to school with black kids before in elementary or middle school, I felt comfortable being with my teammates as a freshman in a school that was very diverse. Maybe it was all the years of *Fresh Prince of Bel-air*, the rap music, or the fact that all the posters in my room were of black athletes. Whatever the reason, I could only see them as I saw myself. It took a while in the high school setting before I realized others did not see my black friends as I did, but it never mattered to me. The black guys on my team had been out to my house several times now and had become my new best friends.

Every time they came to my house, though, my dad was never there. They asked about him, but I just made excuses for his absence. Then one day we had a school project and two of my black friends stayed at my house during the week, and my dad didn't come home. One of my friends kept laughing and saying, "Where's Bob?"

The next day before practice we were all putting our equipment on, and my friend started laughing and said, "Adam, where was Bob last night?" Suddenly and out of nowhere a group of my black friends surrounded me, and it was really quiet in this little huddle. These were some tough dudes, a few were known gang members and head knockers in the school. One of them simply said, "Adam, it's okay. None of us have our dads either." In that moment I realized that I could make it without my dad and that not having him around was okay. I also felt a connection with people other than my family like I had never felt. I realized I could find my own family.

ACCEPTING YOUR REALITY

MANdentity men accept responsibility.

"Whoever conceals his transgressions will not prosper, but he who confesses and forsakes them will obtain mercy."
(Proverbs 28:13 ESV)

We begin our journey to MANdentity by *admitting*. It is time to admit the truth. Have you ever broken a bone or known someone who broke a bone? Once while wrestling with a friend I broke a small bone at the end of my left ring finger. Stubborn and unwilling to go see a doctor, my bone eventually healed in the wrong position. To this day I am unable to fully clinch my fist. To heal correctly, a broken bone must be rightly aligned and held in the correct position.

Many people who seek healing refuse to admit they have a problem. It's similar to my refusing to admit I had a broken bone. Until you admit that there is a problem, proper healing cannot begin. It's time to *admit* the truth of your struggle. Jesus told the religious leaders of the day, 'It is not those who are well who need a doctor, but those who are sick. I didn't come to call the righteous, but sinners" (Mark 2:17 CSB).

When you are actively living in a struggle it's hard to see yourself as you truly are. A struggle is a spiritual, emotional, and physical stronghold that causes wounds from which one desires to break free. Often it takes loved ones or perhaps authority figures in your life to begin uncovering your denial. Days, months, or maybe years of denying your struggle takes a toll on your life. Your refusal to *admit* the truth of your struggle comes at a cost. You may lose your family, friends, health, and even freedoms. The apostle James said: "Do not merely listen to the word, and so deceive yourselves. Do what it says. Anyone who listens to the word but does not do what it says is like someone who looks at his face in a mirror and, after looking at himself, goes away and immediately forgets what he looks like" (James 1:22-24).

You might find yourself unable or unwilling to *admit* the truth about what brought you to this point. Stepping out of denial and admitting your inability to manage your struggle is the beginning of finding healing. This is not to admit defeat but rather to admit a need for help in overcoming this struggle.

One of the ways our enemy, Satan, tries to keep us from admitting our struggle is by convincing us that we can have a life of freedom while actively participating in our struggle. Satan wants us to believe that we can heal and still do the same things we did before. This is a lie Satan uses to trick us. The illusion that one day we will have peace and freedom without changing anything is an age-old trick of the enemy. This lie works exceptionally well with men because deep down we want to overcome the challenges we face on our own power, on our own merit without admitting we need to change. The opportunity to take credit for bringing ourselves out of the struggle we are in looks so good to the heart of a man. It's enticing to our ego and pulls at our pride. If we are ever to change, we first have to admit to ourself that our old way of thinking, our old way of living, our old way of addressing conflict, our old way of connecting with the people around us, and our old way of experiencing God will not work. We must never forget that Satan, the father of lies, is attempting to bait us into thinking we can return to our old ways without really changing. That this time things will work out better even though we haven't done the work to change. Remember how Jesus describes the character of Satan in the Gospel of John: "You belong to your father, the devil, and you want to carry out your father's desires. He was a murderer from the beginning, not holding to the truth, for there is no truth in him. When he lies, he speaks his native language, for he is a liar and the father of lies" (John 8:44). Admitting the truth is the beginning of healing the wounded man within us.

When we *admit* to our innermost self that this struggle is real and that we must not participate in it anymore or act like the wound isn't there, resolving that it only makes everything in our lives worse, only then can we begin working toward a life full of freedom.

Let's begin the process of accepting our reality by facing the truth of our present circumstances.

Make a list of all the ways your life is unmanageable and why. Be specific.

_____

_____

_____

_____

How did you typically handle pain in the past?

_____

_____

_____

_____

_____

Are there areas in your life in which you need to face the truth and admit your struggle?

_____

_____

_____

_____

_____

How do you think admitting your struggle will help you?

_____

_____

_____

_____

_____

Admitting your struggle does not bring condemnation.

"Therefore, there is now no condemnation for those who are in Christ Jesus" (Romans 8:1).

An auto-stereogram is a single-image stereogram, designed to create the visual illusion of a three-dimensional scene from a two-dimensional image. In 1838, the British scientist Charles Wheatstone published an explanation arising from differences in the horizontal positions of images in the two eyes. One can stare at an image and over a matter of seconds the image will transform into something else. At the beginning the image appears to be fuzzy dots and lines crammed together all over. After staring long enough another object begins to appear, such as the face of a woman or a horse. It is important that we view ourselves in the beginning of our recovery the way God views us. Our past mistakes tend to distort our view of how God truly sees us. It's imperative that we keep in mind that admitting your struggle or wound does not bring condemnation from God.

The enemy desires to defeat us and get us to see ourselves as failures. He makes us think about the "what ifs" or "if onlys." He attempts to cloud our hope with worry, regret, and fear from our past failures. It is clear in Scripture that we are not condemned by our past mistakes. Condemnation is a tool Satan uses to keep us stuck in guilt and shame. Guilt and shame tell us that we are not worthy of healing and that deep down we don't deserve help. Satan wants us to judge ourselves harshly and to carry the burden of guilt and shame all alone. This is merely another one of his lies to keep the truth of God's grace away. Conviction is the Holy Spirit prompting us to change, urging us in truth and loving us all the way. It is saturated in grace, which is His unmerited favor. The Creator of the universe came to set us free from our sin. We are not defined by our past, but we need to understand our brokenness in order to grow into the people of God we are called to become. We are like the lost sheep in the parable told by Jesus:

> Now the tax collectors and sinners were all gathering around to hear Jesus. But the Pharisees and the teachers of the law muttered, "This man welcomes sinners and eats with them." Then Jesus told them this parable: "Suppose one of you has a hundred sheep and loses one of them. Doesn't he leave the ninety-nine in the open country and go after the lost sheep until he finds it? And when he finds it, he joyfully puts it on his shoulders and goes home. Then he calls his friends and neighbors together and says, 'Rejoice with me; I have found my lost sheep.' I tell you that in the same way there will be more rejoicing in heaven over one sinner who repents than over ninety-nine righteous persons who do not need to repent." (Luke 15:1-7)

Jesus faced persecution for spending time with people who struggled with sin and were utterly despised. In this moment, He revealed to us a divine insight, specifically, into Gods perspective on our own personal struggles. Imagine a holy man, a man of renown moral character, inviting into his home for dinner people known for committing evil acts, people who are viewed as great sinners. This is exactly what Jesus did, except for one major difference, Jesus wasn't just a holy man, Jesus is God! When you admit your struggle, He rejoices! God is the number one fan of people who repent. He longs for you to admit your struggle and get the help you need. Don't hold anything back. God loves you and wants to support you, not to condemn you.

How has shame impacted your ability to admit your struggle?

Past:

_____

_____

_____

_____

_____

Present:

_____

_____

_____

_____

_____

Admitting your struggle means giving up your pride.

"Pride goes before destruction, a haughty spirit before a fall"
(Proverbs 16:18).

Years ago I hopped in the back of a small Geo Prizm just after work to catch a ride home with a young lady who worked with me. Her brother was crammed in the back seat with me, I had only been a Christian and living a life focused on healing for a few months. I began to ask him about his likes and dislikes in order to grow acquainted with each other. He seemed almost shocked that I was interested in him and was attempting to connect on a personal level. Mid-conversation he abruptly stopped me and asked, "You really don't remember me?"

"No," I sheepishly admitted.

He went on to describe a time in our high school days when I had bullied him. It was one of the most humiliating and humbling moments of my Christian life. I am so thankful God allowed me to catch a glimpse of what I used to be like because that humbling moment motivated me to grow into something better. It wasn't so much the shame of the bullying that humbled me or brought on my willingness to admit my inner most struggles, though. It was the understanding that God loved me despite my sinfulness, that He still wanted me even though I was wretched! In spite of my sin, God wants me, and He wants you too. The understanding of God's grace is what nudged me to change, and I hope it does the same for you. If the grace I speak of sounds to good to be true, then your beginning to understand the grace God has for you.

> "There is nothing concealed that will not be disclosed, or hidden that will not be made known. What you have said in the dark will be heard in the daylight, and what you have whispered in the ear in the inner rooms will be proclaimed from the roofs." —Luke 12:2-3

Pride leads us to a place of destructive behavior. It's counterpart, humility, is the very thing that brings us to a place of constructive behavior. Our selfishness, pride, and ego prevent us from moving forward to find victory over our struggle. One of the tools necessary for emotional and spiritual healing is to learn how to step out of the denial of our past pride and into the humble truth of today's struggles.

In what ways has your pride stopped you from getting the help you need to overcome your struggle?

_____

_____

_____

_____

_____

_____

_____

Healing begins with admitting to ourself that we cannot continue to live in our sin. In your own words, explain why you can never indulge (not even a little) in your struggle anymore?

_____

_____

_____

_____

_____

Admitting your struggle transfers power from us to God.

"I do not understand what I do. For what I want to do I do not do, but what I hate I do. And if I do what I do not want to do, I agree that the law is good. As it is, it is no longer I myself who do it, but it is sin living in me." (Romans 7:15)

The healing begins when we admit our struggle. This requires that we admit our tendency to do the wrong thing and that left to our own devices, apart from God and from people that love and support us in our sin, we will turn back to our struggle.

In the early 1950s there was a family walking in the heat of the day. As they came down the hill of a dirt road, thirsty and hot, the father noticed a man pumping water in the distance on the hillside. As they got closer and closer, he marveled at how consistently the man pumped the water. Wiping the sweat from his brow, the man turned to his wife and said, "What kind of power does a man have to have to pump like that, especially in this heat?" Reaching the base of the hill the family got a better view of the pump and saw what they thought was a man was really an iron cut out attached to a spring. The man turned back to his wife and said, "The man isn't pumping the water. The water is pumping the man." This is exactly what happens when we surrender our struggle to the power of Jesus Christ. It transfers our limited power to Him, and in turn we receive His unlimited power to overcome our struggle.

> Matthew 19:26 "Jesus looked at them and said, "With man this is impossible, but with God all things are possible."

Thankfully we never have to live in our own power anymore. We can choose to surrender our struggle, our life, and our soul over to the care of God. Separation from God feels very real, but it doesn't have to be forever. We may do things that break our fellowship with God, like a child who disobeys his parents, but it's important to remember nothing can separate us from the love of God, just like nothing a child can do will change who their parents are.

"For I am convinced that neither death nor life, neither angels nor demons, neither the present nor the future, nor any powers, neither height nor depth, nor anything else in all creation, will be able to separate us from the love of God that is in Christ Jesus our Lord." (Romans 8:38-39)

What can you do to get closer to God?

_____

_____

_____

_____

_____

2
FINDING THE POWER

It was a comfortable morning in July. The cool breeze and low temperature were a gift to say the least. The sounds of morning competed with my meditation music that played softly in the background as I journaled. The sound of the owl saying farewell for the morning took me back to memories of lying in my bed deep in the country as a kid. I'd hear an owl just outside the window of our double-wide trailer as I debated rising out of my comfy bed littered with stuffed animals, although I knew nothing but adventure awaited me. My mom and father, if he happened to be home, would still be passed out from their drinking the night before. I would be free to explore the creeks in the woods surrounding our little property. I would spend hours running through the woods with my dog, Smokey, and walking along the creaks checking for frogs and tiny crawfish hiding under rocks. I get emotional when I think about Smokey and how I came back home one day and found him dead, most likely from starvation. He was neglected. My mother was addicted to pills. My father had left. My brother had moved to college, and I... well, I had run away.

I ran to get away, to get away from the pain I felt, but everywhere I went it followed. I suspect many can relate to attempting to running away from themselves to no avail. I ended up finishing high school and made it into college—one semester at least. One semester of drinking until the sun came up and sleeping until the sun went down. I was miserable but too proud to admit it or show it. Out of control is the only way to describe my lifestyle as a nineteen-year-old kid left to fend for himself. I was attempting to heal the wounds by filling the void with alcohol, drugs, and sex. The college dorm room was the perfect place for me to hide out and fumble my way through life while avoiding the pain deep inside. It was sort of a playground in which I played life. I acted like things were important, like I cared, like things mattered. But in reality I was numb, trying to feel with broken connections. I don't know what my response would have been if asked to describe how I felt or about my faith. Simply put, I had none. There had been no faith or healthy emotional connections in my home growing up.

As a nineteen-year-old freshman in college, inside I was broken and disconnected from reality. I didn't know how to express my feelings. I'm not even sure if I could explain what emotions were. The moments when I did try to share my feelings, I flew into a rage. I was like a small boat being broken apart on the mountainous seas of life. Barely floating, tossed from side to side with no plan, purpose, or course in mind.

Desperate for a change and drowning in the depths of my soul, I thought spring break was my life preserver. In the 1990s MTV's show *Spring Break* dominated. It was the self-proclaimed getaway for tired and overly busy college students. It was an escape from being the people we were exhausted from pretending to be. In fact, most of my life was exhausting for that very reason. I was tired of pretending to be someone I thought others would like or others wanted me to be. I had lost my ability to feel what was real. Reality was fragmented because I experienced it with a broken emotional perspective. Each time I was hurt, disappointed, confused, curious, or feeling lost no one was there to help. I felt rejected, abandoned, and learned to stuff my feelings. I didn't have any tools to cope with life in a healthy way. This prevented me from having deep connections with others and with God. Think of a flashlight with a battery slowly losing power. It flickers at first, gets dimmer and dimmer, then it goes off only to be back on in a few seconds. Eventually the lights out for good. Its owner smacks it hoping to rattle some power from inside the depleted batteries.

There were a few people who noticed my batteries were losing their juice. One such person was a precious girlfriend of mine in high school. At that point she was the only person in my life who had a capacity to truly love and the only person that exemplified a healthy relationship with God. She did everything in her power to help me and tried to love me with all her heart, but since I had no idea why my light was going out, there was nothing she could do to help me. I'd have a ball of emotional pain in my stomach, and I wouldn't know how to tell her. My throat would constrict, and I wanted desperately to share with her my feelings, but I didn't know how to put them into words. *Why can't I just simply love her and share my heart with her?* I screamed at myself. There is nothing more painful than deeply loving someone and not being able to deeply express your love.

This had been the pattern of my life in most of my relationships. I'd been a fading flashlight for far too long. I deeply desired to shine brightly with love. Instead I'd express a flicker of kindness, then get dim when I'd lash out when feeling exposed or threatened. The light was out, and I ran, trying to hide from the guilt and confusion of my feelings. As I said, this is a miserable place to be, desiring to love but not knowing how and being so damaged that you can't.

The first chance I had I ran! I ran from the pain, the past, the hurt, the anger, the hopelessness, I ran from people who knew me enough to get close. I was tired of marveling at people with balanced lives, people capable of genuinely smiling, truly loving, and actually enjoying life. When I say marvel, I mean marvel. I think of a girl from my high school who I had gotten close with during my senior year. Her smile was as bright as the sun. She had a centeredness about her that intrigued me. I loved just being in her presence, chatting on her couch next to the Christmas tree, laughing and enjoying our time, but her genuine love for life and herself also confused me because at that point I was incapable of such inner peace.

So there I was running away from myself. I headed out for spring break with a suitcase full of clothes, twenty dollars, and two of my party buddies. We stole gas along the way to Florida and slept in my 1989 LTD. Waves of college students would arrive from different states ready to let loose and detach from all the stress of life. They would stay only for a week and then go back to their parents or college to those who loved them. I stayed in Florida, living in my LTD for the next ten months. I was like a Zoologist studying wild animals, hoping to extract some sort of knowledge that would help me become a part of the herd. I was seeking to be normal, but there was absolutely nothing normal about my emotional development and trauma; it was destructive and harmful. I assumed that the solution was outside of myself, that it was something I needed to learn from them and apply to myself.

It took me a while, but I finally discovered that the healing I had been searching for was deep inside of me. The only way to find it was through my past, and I couldn't go alone. I found a magnificent God who wanted to go with me, and he wants to go with you too. With Him and the help of some trusted others, you can find healing just as I did.

FINDING THE POWER

MANdentity men rely on God's strength above their own.

"Trust in the LORD forever, for the LORD GOD is an everlasting rock." (Isaiah 26:4)

We experience many things we cannot see with our eyes but still have evidence of their existence. Hebrews 11:1 says that "faith is the substance of things hoped for, the evidence of things not seen." The wind is a good example. We cannot see wind, but we can see evidence all around that it exists. I'll never forget the first time I drove through a large subdivision that had recently been devastated by a tornado. It resembled a landfill. Trees were broken off just above the base of the trunk, piles of the debris was everywhere, and there was little to indicate it had once been a place inhabited by families grilling in the backyard or kids playing in the streets. Our sin often brings us to a similar place. It's as if we are driving through the wreckage of our lives looking from a car window in awe at the devastation. How did this happen? Who did this? The car comes to a halt and we realize the tornado was our behavior, our actions, our choices, or perhaps the tornado had simply happened to us with no fault of our own. Although we may not be able see the wind of a tornado, we can most definitely see its results. In some cases we were the tornado and in others the tornado was someone or something else. Either way, the cleanup rests on our shoulders.

First, we have to admit the reality of our struggle. This is exactly where many of us find ourselves. It can be a scary moment. *How did I do this?* you might be asking. *How did I get here?* We must take an honest assessment of the wreckage, and it's important we admit our responsibility for the wreckage. But it's also important we don't get caught staring out the window too long. This can lead us back into the same tornado.

Like the wind we may not be able to physically touch God, but His presence in our lives is palpable. One of the names of God is *Jehovah Shammah*, which means "Jehovah is there." It means in the Hebrew culture that God is with you. As we look over some pains from our past and the difficulties of our struggles, we must make sure to understand that God is with us. God is with you! MANdentity men practice this belief each day.

"Have I not commanded you? Be strong and courageous. Do not be afraid; do not be discouraged, for the Lord your God will be with you wherever you go." (Joshua 1:9)

"Fear not, for I am with you; be not dismayed, for I am your God; I will strengthen you, I will help you, I will uphold you with my righteous right hand." (Isaiah 41:10)

"I am with you always, to the very end of the age." (Matthew 28:20)

How have you struggled to believe in God in your past? Do you have any fears or doubts about your faith in God?

_____

_____

_____

How would having a closed mind be harmful to your spiritual growth?

_____

_____

_____

In your own words, who is God?

_____

_____

_____

Often the people in our lives can affect our belief in God negatively or positively. How have your feelings about God been impacted by the people in your life?

_____

_____

_____

MANdentity men have faith in Jesus Christ's power to save.

"For I am not ashamed of the gospel, for it is the power of God for salvation" (Romans 1:16)

Faith is often misunderstood. Many people have determined that faith is a decision that comes with the absence of doubt, fear, and worry. We must understand as believers in Christ that our faith is a journey not a singular moment. Faith in God grows as we grow over time. However, no one ever finished a journey they did not first start. Now is the time to begin your journey of faith in the right direction with Jesus Christ.

God the Father knew that we could never be perfect; it is impossible. After Adam and Eve disobeyed God in the garden, every human on earth was born with a sin nature, which is why we don't have to train toddlers to be selfish. "For all have sinned and fall short of the glory of God" (Romans 3:23). No human is perfect, but God is.

There are consequences to sin, though. Many of us have faced the aftermath of our sin struggles. But there is no greater spiritual consequence to sin then spending an eternity separated from God: "For the wages of sin is death, but the gift of God is eternal life in Christ Jesus our Lord" (Romans 6:23). The death the apostle Paul refers to here is a second death, a spiritual death not our physical death. When our physical bodies die, our soul lives on forever either with God or apart from God. Our salvation is not staked on our moral character. It's not a spiritually weighted scale of our good deeds and our bad deeds that determines our eternity with God or apart from Him. It's solely based on the work Christ has done on the cross for those who put their faith in Him. This is why God sent His son Jesus Christ to earth for us. God came to us because we could not work our way to a state of perfection before Him.

———

"He made Him who knew no sin to be sin on our behalf, so that we might become the righteousness of God in Him." (2 Corinthians 5:21 NASB)

The Bible tells us

- Jesus lived a sinless life while on earth.

- Jesus died on the cross for the sins of the world.

- Jesus rose again three days later ultimately conquering the penalty of sin.

- If you will repent of your sin (repenting is acknowledging before God that you are a sinner), believe in the sinless sacrifice of Jesus Christ on the cross and in the Power that raised Him from the dead and then if you will receive the gift of salvation, you will be saved.

Earthly healing and eternal life with God begin with placing your faith in Jesus Christ for salvation. God sent His son Jesus to earth for you. If you want to place your faith in Jesus Christ for salvation and begin your journey to healing now, here is how. Find solitude with just you and God in the space you are in. Tell God of your sin, hold nothing back, and express your remorse and willingness to admit all your sin. Tell God that you believe that Jesus Christ is the Son of God and that you believe in His sacrifice on the cross for your sin. Tell God you believe that Jesus rose from the dead and conquered the penalty of sin. Ask God to come inside your heart and save your soul. Stop reading and pray.

———

Have you ever surrendered your life to Jesus Christ? If so, write a brief testimony of the moment you came to faith in Jesus? Especially if you just surrendered your life to Jesus after reading the paragraphs above. Write what brought you to this decision.

_____

_____

_____

_____

_____

_____

_____

_____

_____

_____

MANdentity men place their Faith in Jesus Christ's power to restore.

"The God of all grace, who called you to his eternal glory in Christ, after you have suffered a little while, will himself restore you and make you strong, firm and steadfast" (1 Peter 5:10)

One of my favorites shows is *Rust Valley Restorers*. The show is based in Canada and the star of the show is Mike. He is an eccentric entrepreneur, hippy capitalist and a rust collector. He has acres of old, beat down, rusted out cars. The show opens with Mike driving through the muddy fields in his tow truck, going from row to row, salivating over the hunks of junk. Suddenly, he slams the brakes and the camera cuts to his old wrecker sliding in the mud, and before you know it Mike is out of the truck raving over a vehicle that has a bird nest under the hood, no motor, only two rims, and is completely unable to function. Mike yells through his grey dreadlocks and tiny eyeglasses with a huge smile, "There's my masterpiece!" Let those words sink into your soul for a moment: "There's my masterpiece."

"I will praise you because I have been remarkably and wondrously made. Your works are wondrous, and I know this very well." (Psalms 139:14 CSB)

When God looks at you that is exactly what He cries out: "My masterpiece!" Mike has a keen ability to restore cars, unlike anyone I've ever seen. But nothing can compare to the restorative power of God. Once we place our faith in God, He goes to work. Trusting in God's power to restore us is the next step in our healing process.

What changes in your thinking and behavior are necessary for your restoration?

Thinking   Behavior

_____   _____

_____   _____

_____   _____

_____   _____

In which areas of your life are you ready to allow God's power to restore you?

_____

_____

_____

_____

3
SURRENDER TO WIN

It was a warm day when I arrived at the duplex where my now wife was staying. With her pregnant belly poking out, she gingerly walked toward the little rubber ball our son was looking for as I pulled up. I spent a little time outside with the both of them shooting basketball on the plastic goal with our one-year-old son. I had one son and another on the way, and all the responsibility that went with that did not even cross my mind. I had no intention of putting anyone else's needs before my own during this season of our lives.

We had just split from living together a week earlier due to my drinking and drug dealing. I had become cold and distant. She could no longer trust anything I did or said. When we had been together, most of our days were spent apart. She was at work, our son was at daycare, and I attended college in the mornings and then sold drugs and drank until it was time to pick up our son in the afternoons. Most nights I was in and out selling and running the streets. Meanwhile, she patiently waited and loved me with all the love she had when I came around. Her lack of love was not the problem; it was me. As a teenager I tried to navigate life without a father and with a drug addicted mother, I was broken. Now with a child of my own and a woman who loved me, those trauma wounds and alcoholism affected my ability to lead a healthy life. The drug dealing and drinking was a way for me to run from God's call on my life and hide from the pain I felt inside. Anything to keep me from thinking about who I had become.

After playing with our son and flirting with his pregnant mother, we headed inside the apartment. As we all walked into the duplex, her phone rang. It was our former landlord, a police officer, asking her to return the keys to the apartment we had rented from him. He wanted to know where she lived so he could come and get the keys, but she was too smart for that. I had left the apartment in bad shape, and the police officer was not happy about it. In my eyes it was all a joke. I had no remorse or sense of accountability. It was how I lived.

I had become a taker and an abuser of anything and everyone. I didn't understand the concept of love, and my application of it was diluted in self-will. I learned how to be a selfish taker by living with a pill addicted mother who spent most of her time using me and her boyfriends to get what she wanted. Kids learn how to love from their parents. The attachments we have with those who raise us ultimately shape the attachments we have with others. For me love meant you would give me what I wanted when I wanted it, and I would do my best to give you what you wanted when you wanted it. The dilemma was that my girlfriend wanted a consistent soul connection with a man. Someone to talk with, laugh with, and share intimate moments with. Unfortunately, the only feelings I knew how to share were lust, anger, and rage.

After several minutes of her talking with our former landlord, I grabbed the phone and let him know that I would deliver the keys sometime that night. After another hour or so I left to make a drug deal and return the keys. As I type this, I'm sickened by the contentment I felt leaving the duplex that day. I left a pregnant woman who loved me with all of her soul and my son who loved me unconditionally as I sought out money, alcohol and sex. I had become my dad to a T. He had walked out on my mom, my brother, and me to party at the lake and live promiscuously with women. The person I resented the most was the person I had become the most like.

Later that night I parked down the street from the apartment. Just a few weeks earlier several drug dealers had been indicted. I was afraid they might be looking for me, so I was driving a different vehicle than normal, staying at another apartment, and making sure not to have much money or drugs on me. I walked in the blackness of the night to place the keys in the mailbox. Its aluminon lid shone in the streetlight. I slowly opened the squeaky door before placing the keys inside, hoping to slip out unnoticed. I quickly hoped in the SUV and sped down the street toward my stash. While giving instructions on my cell to my next client, I noticed a police car speeding fast behind me. Believing it was the landlord ready to give me a piece of his mine, I got off the phone and did my best to abide by all the traffic laws. After a few miles I decided to make a turn and see if he was intent on following me. I quickly turned into a McDonald's, and he hit his blue lights. Stopping right in the middle of the drive through, the young cop walked fast to my door carrying a stack of papers in his hand. The window on the SUV did not work, so I opened the door to explain the window. He interrupted me. "Are you Adam French?" he asked. "Yes," I responded. "Mr. French, we have several indictments for your arrest." He placed me in handcuffs, searched my person, and quickly began sharing his find over the radio in the front seat. As I sat in the back, my phone, which was on the console in the front was ringing over and over again as the client was wondering about my delay. The name "Snow White" continued to appear. Finally, the officer grabbed my phone and powered it off. I've never received another call for drugs or anything illegal since. For some reason, a sense of release came over me. It was over. I could power off now.

SURRENDER TO WIN

MANdentity men surrender their will over to Christ's will.

"I have been crucified with Christ and I no longer live, but Christ lives in me. The life I now live in the body, I live by faith in the Son of God, who loved me and gave himself for me."
(Galatians 2:20)

The greatest decision a man can make is to surrender his will to the care of Jesus Christ. In sports, business, personal wealth, relationships, and in Western culture in general, winning is paramount. We are taught to win at all costs. Whether it's the dad screaming at his four-year-old son's T-ball coach or the mom confronting the referee after her five-year-old daughter's first soccer game, many of us act as though we should be winning at all cost. It's safe to say that in our modern world, nothing matters more to a man than winning! Don't get me wrong, I'm not suggesting that men should be okay with losing. Winning is a good goal to have, but I am asking you to consider a different perspective on winning.

Winning takes on an entirely different meaning in the providence of God. His thoughts are not like our thoughts, and His design for living and winning is different than what culture teaches us. Winning is not just the score; it's not just the wins and losses.

I'm not for everyone getting a trophy or removing the score. We must learn that sometimes we win and sometimes we lose. The principle that matters the most in competition or in striving for success, though, is learning what winning actually looks like in each situation we face. We have been taught to pull ourselves up by our own bootstraps. That the will of a man determines his success and a "how many punches can a man take without giving up" type of belief system is engrained in us through movies, music, and sometimes even by our own families. But in God's economy of winning, when we surrender to the care of God, we win! Surrender to win is the framework in which God restores and provides healing in our struggles. Jesus told us that if we love Him, we will keep His commandments. In other words, He's saying that our love encompasses more than a feeling; it also renders a posture of humility and obedience to His teaching.

"Humble yourselves before the Lord, and He will lift you up." (James 4:10)

Surrender is not to be offered reluctantly as the defeated general submits to his conqueror, but voluntarily as a patient on the operating table submits to the skilled hand of the surgeon who wields the knife. MANdentity men cease fighting the solution that God has presented before us. We become our own worst enemy when we oppose the idea of surrendering our entire lives over to Christ's care. God loves us enough to provide solutions to our emotional and spiritual struggles. When we continue to do it our way and resist the idea of surrendering, we are literally squaring off against God. I finally came to a place where I was tired of fighting against God in the ring of life when I heard my two-year-old son call out, "Daddy!" through the jail phone. That painful moment broke me.

Merriam-Webster defines *surrender* as yielding to "the power, control, or possession of another." When we actively participate in our sin, we resist the will of God for our lives and oppose His purpose for our lives. Every man has a wound. Every man needs help. Every man has something to surrender. God extends his mighty and gracious hand to all men. Our part is to surrender our will over to His care and then we begin winning. There is nothing more warming to the heart of God when a man gives his life completely over to His care. We were designed to worship, obey and be in relationship with our creator. The greatest decision a man can make is to surrender his will over to the care of Jesus Christ. You don't have to live alone with your struggles anymore. There is an unprecedented hope in the strong loving arm of Jesus and now is your time to surrender to win.

"For if, while we were God's enemies, we were reconciled to Him through the death of his Son, how much more, having been reconciled, shall we be saved through his life!" (Romans 5:10)

Our struggles put us at odds with all the good and perfect gifts God has for us. Admitting we have a sin problem and placing our faith in God brings us to the reality about who we are and how our struggle has affected our life. It's been said that the farther down sin takes you, the better chance you have at finding healing because coming to that place of incomprehensible demoralization, or hitting rock bottom, provides the willingness needed to surrender all to Christ. As the old hymn goes, "All to Jesus I surrender, All to Him I freely give, I will ever love and trust Him, In His presence daily live." For years, my wife and I struggled with intimacy. For me intimacy meant how well I was performing in bed. For her intimacy was about meeting each other's emotional and spiritual needs. This concept was foreign to me and something I was unwilling to surrender. Refusing to accept any fault in this area and unwilling to acknowledge I could be wrong only drove a larger wedge between us. I was afraid to admit that I couldn't truly connect with her emotionally. I didn't know how. I was operating in my own will with my old past hurts, my old dysfunctional view of relationships and unwilling to seek help. It wasn't until I surrendered my struggle over to Jesus and started practicing humility with her did things begin to improve. My wife would tell me how much she loved and so desperately wanted to connect with me emotionally. In frustration I reminded her of all the good things that I was doing for her and the kids. All I needed to do was admit that I could not do it on my own. I needed help from God and from others to grow in this area. MANdentity is about learning to surrender our wills over to the care of Jesus Christ. There will be many areas as you grow in your faith that will require this practice.

> "No one can take my life from me. I sacrifice it voluntarily. For I have the authority to lay it down when I want to and also to take it up again. For this is what my Father has commanded." (John 10:18)

Just as Christ voluntarily surrendered to the cross, we have the same opportunity to surrender our struggle over to His care. In the cross, God poured out His grace, His unmerited favor. God gives us favor not because of something we have done, but because of what He has done. Eternal salvation is a one-time decision, but the healing process is cultivated through a conscious daily surrender to God.

When I admitted that I needed help and chose to place my faith in Jesus Christ who alone had the power to restore me; then my healing began. If you have done this, now you can begin the practice of turning your will over to His will each day. No one hits rock bottom or finds themselves in the middle of a struggle on accident. Our own selfishness, unwillingness to ask for help, and reluctance to turn our will over is what got us into our mess in the first place. It is important that we begin to seek the will of God and His understanding by surrendering our will to His care. Now is the time for you to surrender your will over to God's care and experience all the healing that comes with it.

List people, places, or things that you need to surrender over to the care of God.

_____

_____

_____

If you surrender all that you wrote above, what are you afraid will happen?

_____

_____

_____

What actions will you take to begin surrendering your will over to the care of God?

_____

_____

_____

Surrender your understanding over to God's care.

"Trust in the Lord with all your heart and lean not on your own understanding; in all your ways submit to him, and he will make your paths straight. Do not be wise in your own eyes; fear the Lord and shun evil. [8] This will bring health to your body and nourishment to your bones" (Proverbs 3:5-8).

In today's world shopping can easily be done from the couch, the front porch, or while riding as a passenger in the car. My wife and I ordered our prescription glasses from an app on our phone in a matter of minutes. Each pair came in less than a week with trendy packaging and sleek designer frames. Putting on a pair of glasses should help you see everything more clearly, but not for my wife. Her glasses made the world around her blurrier. It was clear the prescription wasn't right. Just like my wife's prescription didn't work for her, in the past when we have been immersed in our struggle, we were viewing the world with glasses not prescribed to us by God but through our own broken perspective. We were not meant to live only by our own understanding and to see things only from our own perspective. This gives us a blurred vision of the world around us and leads us to a life of struggle.

When we try to overcome by only our own understanding, we alienate everyone and everything that is trying to help us. This is another tool of Satan to isolate us and rob us from a life richly connected to the truths of Scripture and from the people who desperately love us. Isolation is a warning sign that our ego, our will, and our own understanding has started to separate us from the people and things that make us healthy. Isolation is a false sense of safety built from a wall of unbiblical understanding. A "my way or the highway" attitude leaves us traveling alone on a one-way street going in the wrong direction. When we isolate, we begin to perceive things differently than they truly are. Satan loves to isolate us, so he can tell us lies that encourage our separation and deepens our brokenness. He uses our past and present hurts to distort our reality, hoping that we will lean on our own understanding and not the understanding God has given us through his Word. Next comes the blame game.

Blame is another trick of Satan. Left to our own understanding, we blame ourselves for things we did not do and blame others for things we did. Our enemy wants to keep us isolated and confused so that we cannot live in the solutions of scripture and in healthy community with others. He wants us to blame others so we can stay stuck in our struggles. When we blame others for our struggles, there is no solution because we don't have the power to change others. We can only change ourselves. I know because I stayed isolated for years. I blamed myself for all the things my parents were responsible for and blamed others for all things I needed to take responsibility for. This type of blame game creates a broken emotional and spiritual cycle. We get trapped by our own broken understanding.

Surrendering our will over to God is like putting on a new pair of glasses with the right prescription and seeing everything more clearly. To accomplish this, we must continue to examine our soul and expose the deep-rooted lies that are preventing us from seeing the truth.

How has following your own will affected your life? How has it affected others?

Past

Present

_____   _____

_____   _____

_____   _____

_____   _____

_____   _____

What would change in your life today if you made the decision to turn your life completely over to Gods will?

_____

_____

_____

_____

"Teach me to do your will, for you are my God; may your good Spirit lead me on level ground." (Psalms 143:10)

God wants to teach us how to live in accordance with His will and understanding. When we align our lives with His will and His understanding, healing takes place and our ability to find freedom from our struggle is not far off. Following the will of God begins as we learn the difference between our will and His. This is why the MANdentity journey is so important for our healing and for our continued growth. Think of it like a chain with knots, kinks, and missing links. A chain like this is unable to function in the way it was designed to function. Another way to put it is the chain is unable to fulfill the purpose for which it was created for because of the damaged shape it is now in. I once was a damaged chain unable to function and fulfill the purpose for which God created me. But now, God who is rich in mercy has given me a new chain, and He is able and willing to do the same for you. The only way He can do that is if you let go of your damaged chain, let go of your life, and place it in His hands.

> "But blessed is the one who trusts in the Lord, whose confidence is in him. They will be like a tree planted by the water that sends out its roots by the stream. It does not fear when heat comes; its leaves are always green. It has no worries in a year of drought and never fails to bear fruit." (Jeremiah 17:7-8)

A daily practice of surrendering helps us to learn to trust God. The nature of surrender is turning over your will, getting out of the way, and being restored to reality, honesty, and a peace of mind through the will of God.

What is the difference between your will and God's will?

Your will:

_____

_____

_____

_____

_____

God's will:

_____

_____

_____

_____

Am I unwilling to do things in my healing process that are being suggested? If so, why?

_____

_____

_____

_____

4
GETTING HONEST

A summer scrimmage between my high school basketball teammates and I seemed harmless until a player from the other scrimmage squad made a threatening remark to me. One of the players
on my team from a different gang affiliation took offense and it es-
calated rapidly into a fight. Add in all the partying I was into, and
it was easy for me to decide to transfer to a school across the state
line. Walking into a new school wasn't really daunting to me. I was
cocky and arrogant. My first locker was on the bottom row, and I
hadn't really thought about it much until this long legged cheer-
leader started wearing skirts . She got my attention, and for the
next three years we were best friends and lovers. When you're sixteen with no father and a drug addicted mother and a brother away
at college, there is lots of alone time. No one checked in on me or
was providing any accountability in my life. This girl tried to fill
those voids. And as hard as I tried to mess it up with my emotional
roller coasters, she would not stop loving and supporting me.

At first we spent most weeknights at her house doing homework, eating dinner with her family, or talking for hours in her room. She was the only stable and secure thing in my life. Over time her stability and security helped me realize my instability and insecurity. If I wasn't with her, I was with my friends smoking weed and drinking or alone in our double-wide trailer deep in the woods. It was the pretending that bothered me so much. Pretending that my life was normal at her dinner table with her parents. Pretending that talking football with her dad and schoolwork with her mom were normal things that I thought about. Pretending that my world matched hers. In reality my home life was very different. My reality was me alone living in a dingy, dusty double-wide trailer in the middle of the country and no one attending my sports games. It was smoking weed in the living room, playing video games, and shooting pistols at trees behind the trailer. Normal for me, if not alone smoking weed and playing video games, was drinking a few beers and smoking weed with my mom's boyfriend. Most days at home I felt alone, empty, and scared. There was a certain heaviness like a cloud of worry hanging over me. In contrast, my girl seemed like an angel in my eyes, and I felt like a devil who was allowed to be influenced by this angelic being.

For months she told me she did not want to have sex, but she never really explained why. I tried everything. I told her if she loved me, she would have sex with me. And I even broke up with her just to try to get my way. One day she picked me up on a Saturday morning and in her genuine misplaced desire to prove her love for me, she folded and agreed to have sex with me.

After that day sex became a regular part of our relationship. As the weeks went on, she continued to mature, flourish, and grow. I continued to grow out of control, diminish, and become reckless in my actions. She did the best to mother me, love me, befriend me, teach me, coach me, and help me with every ounce of her soul, but she was fighting a losing battle. Into our senior year and as the future after high school was looming, I could sense she was slowly slipping away. The movie of her in college was easy to watch, but when I played my movie, I couldn't even see myself alive. My late nights had become more frequent. I was late to school every day and was using drugs and drinking every day.

One day while having sex at my house, I purposely tried getting her pregnant—another selfish decision by a broken, neglected, and hopeless teenage boy. Looking back at our relationship now, I believed that she would leave me at some point. She had it all, and I had nothing else. She was the only thing I had that was good. I didn't plan it out. It was a split-second decision by a boy desperate for love and attention. A decision that led me to an even darker place.

She called me one night crying and told me she was pregnant. I had been out drinking and smoking with my friends alone as she told me the news, I was bitter, numb, and disgusted with my life. I remember when she called not being able to feel anything, and my response was to break up with her and hang up. I can remember the terror of not being able to feel anything in that moment. Emotionally numb, physically alone and lost spiritually. I didn't answer her calls or speak to her for two weeks. She called for about a week and then the calls stopped. That wasn't the first time I had played roller-coaster with our relationship and with her heart. Throughout our relationship, I would say mean things to her, break up with her, and then be as sweet as I could to express my true love for her.

Hurt people hurt people because they don't know any other way to deal with the pain. That is how I treated her. After two weeks, I got a call from her that I just randomly decided to answer. She told me that her mom took her away, and she got an abortion. "Why?" I responded. "Because," she said through tears. "Adam! You broke up with me and I didn't know what to do, so I told my mom." The way she said my name pierced my soul. She yelled with a brokenness that I never wanted her to feel but could never express from my own heart. I can still hear her voice if I think hard enough; some things we never forget. A part of me died and for years I wasn't the same after that moment. All hope in me was lost. I've never for one second resented her decision. I blamed myself. I felt deep down that I was not good enough to have a child, and it wasn't until I began honestly sharing stories like these did my self-worth and healing come.

GETTING HONEST

MANdentity men are honest with themselves, others, and God.

"Having put away falsehood, let each one of you speak the truth with his neighbor, for we are members one of another."
(Ephesians 4:25 ESV)

Having a family now is one of the greatest joys of my life, but it comes with lots of unexpected challenges. There are five of us, and it is a challenge to keep clothes washed, folded, and put away in our home. My wife and I wash and fold clothes, but inevitably somewhere in our home there's a random piece of dirty clothing tucked away. Imagine walking into your bedroom and clothes are thrown everywhere. Conducting an honest search of your heart can feel like walking into a room full of dirty clothes. The thing about dirty clothes is that we are the ones who keep piling them up. For years many of us have let our resentments, our fears and our pain pile up.

You may have asked yourself one of these questions: How did this happen? Whose fault is this? Where do I go from here? To put it simply, MANdentity men must get completely honest. The reality is we may not actually know how some of the pieces of dirty clothes got in our lives. This is what the MANdentity book is all about. In order for you to move toward healing and to find freedom from your struggle, you must be honest. We are afforded the privilege of inventorying our heart. It will take a few chapters to begin journeying through our hearts, but the reward far outweighs the effort required.

"Search me, God, and know my heart; test me and know my anxious thoughts. See if there is any offensive way in me, and lead me in the way everlasting." (Psalms 139:23-24)

The first time I flew on an airplane I was twenty-two years old. I was on my way to Santa Clara, California, to attend Bible college. It was like I floated out there, like I was on top of the world. Jesus had become my life and I loved anything and everything about His ministry. Upon arriving at the Bible college, someone handed me a small book with 375 rules. If I broke any of the rules, I would get demerits, and if I had too many demerits, I would be kicked out. Little did I know, I had ventured into a community that resembled a cult more than a group of believers following Scripture.

Armed with less than two years of Bible knowledge after a radical salvation, I dove headfirst into their teaching. My first chapel service was confusing and shocking. Several men were sitting on a platform. They were wearing suits and all their haircuts were exactly the same. One man stood up and yelled for thirty plus minutes denouncing, or I should say demonizing, the wearing of blue jeans and make-up by woman, going to the movies, music that was not produced from their community, and all versions of the Bible except the King James Version. I brushed it off and chose to stay focused on my opportunity to learn the Bible, get equipped, and one day plant a church that could change the world.

The longer I stayed the more discrepancies I found between their teaching and what was in Scripture. In my mind, I had done everything possible to become one of them. I wore only suits with ties. My hair had a hard part with shiny gel, and I carried a list of things not to do in my heart that displayed my closeness to God. Eventually I found myself in a place of deep shame and guilt, which I had mistaken for spiritual conviction.

While visiting a girlfriend in Tarzana, California, to meet her family, I held her hand and hugged her. Upon returning to school, I realized that I had broken some of the rules of the Bible College. Students were supposed to stay at least six inches away from any-one of the opposite sex for fear of sexual sin. I had been elected the chaplain of my grade and had a deep since of shame and guilt over my transgression. The thought of sinning against God was so overwhelming that I had trouble sleeping and began to experience bouts of anxiousness. I requested a meeting with the president of the school. With my head hanging low, I confessed to holding hands and hugging my girlfriend. The president of the college, who I had heard himself condemn such behavior from the pulpit, laughed in my face. He said, "If you hadn't of held her hand or hugged her, then we might have a problem." Then he suggested something about not being homosexual and totally disregarded my confession.

Coming from a world of sex, drugs, and alcohol before my salvation, my heart was damaged from my past, and the legalistic pressure exhausted my soul. The guilt and shame that brought me to confess to the school president immediately turned to anger. Barely containing the rage burning inside of me, I stood and shook his hand and smiled in his face, just like they had taught me. I left his office to never return. I felt so foolish, hurt, and confused. It was like God had removed the scales from my eyes as he did for Saul. There were many standards they taught but never expected us to keep. Here I was depriving myself and struggling to follow all the rules, believing with all my heart that God expected such behavior, only to find out it was all pharisaical.

My next flight home felt more like I was under the world than on top of it. I was so hurt and resented God for allowing me to experience such a place. I had lost my passion for Jesus Christ and gained a resentment towards the Church. *How could you send me to a place like that God?* I thought. *Why would you allow me to go there, God?* Some of you can relate. Maybe you have deep-rooted resentments at God or the Church for all that you or your loved ones have been through. We all must honestly search our hearts to find the pain, the resentment, and other things that are robbing us from the peace that we so desire, the peace Christ promised to leave us.

> "Peace I leave with you; my peace I give to you. Not as the world gives do I give to you. Let not your hearts be troubled, neither let them be afraid." (John 14:27)

The prophet Jeremiah tells us to "examine our ways and test them, and let us return to the LORD" (Lamentations 3:40). This is where the rubber meets the road, and we begin to move forward in our healing process. It's time to slowly sift through the wreckage of our past. The important thing to keep in our hearts during this process is that there's no wrong way to do it except for not to do it. Think of it like cleaning a house. If you came to my house and cleaned, it would not be important to me where you started or how you specifically did it; I just want the house to be clean. This lesson on honesty teaches us how to clean house. Honesty is about being willing to look at your part in the resentments, fears, and pains we have. Honesty is not just about examining what others have done to you. It's also about searching your heart and exposing your own sin and struggles so that you can heal. When you accept responsibility for your part, the stronghold of your struggle can be broken, and you start to grow into a healthy place and discover your true MANdentity.

In what areas or relationships in your life have you been selfish, dishonest, and self-seeking?

I've been selfish:

_____

_____

_____

_____

I've been dishonest:

_____

_____

_____

_____

What people, places, or things do you resent and what led to those resentments?

_____

_____

_____

What have you done to allow your resentments to build up?

_____

_____

_____

How have your resentments affected your life, your relationships with others and yourself?

_____

_____

_____

By facing the pain, we caused and the pain we experienced, we find the starting place for our spiritual growth and healing. It's important that you "guard your heart, for everything you do flows from it" (Proverbs 4:23). We learn how to guard our own hearts by understanding the pain we've caused others, or the pain others have caused us. This helps us understand our tendency to act out from places of resentment, fear, and hurt. Resentment and fear are often one of the causes of our struggles.

Think of it like this, God designed our brains for loving connection with Him and others. When our experiences with God and others is not loving and brings pain, we desire to find ways to comforts ourselves. We seek out alternative ways to get the love we were created to give and receive. As we search for loving connection outside of Gods design, we are hurt, and we hurt others. Many of us turn to drugs, sex, pornography, gambling, rage, or become workaholics. We may also develop other emotional issues such as anxiety or depression. Many spiritual struggles are rooted in resentment and fear. Let's clean house and gain tools to properly guard against such behaviors in the future by honestly inspecting our hearts.

About whom or from what do you feel ashamed or guilty?

_____

_____

_____

What feelings do you have the most trouble allowing yourself to feel?

_____

_____

_____

Why?

_____

_____

_____

How have you acted out your feelings destructively in the past?

_____

_____

_____

In the present?

_____

_____

_____

When my father first purchased our land, he cleared several acres of trees with his bulldozer, leaving massive piles of wood for us to burn. These enormous wood piles were transformed into army bases, playgrounds, and a test of our courage. I'll never forget the day our neighbor's grandson, Noels, came over to build forts with my brother and me. We were standing on the highest point of the pile. Noels was in front of me, and I started saying, "Jump! Jump!

Chicken! What? Are you scared? Are you afffraaaiiid?" Suddenly, he jumped, and all I heard was him screaming. Covered up with some of the brush at the base of our landing spot was an old tractor disc. A tractor disc is used to plow up the dirt when preparing it for planting crops. It's a heavy steel piece of equipment with sharp metal discs on one end. When Noels landed on it, it deeply cut both of his legs. Sometimes jumping into the unknown is an act of foolishness, as in Noels case, and other times taking a leap of faith into the unknown is an act of obedience. An honest examination of our hearts feels like stepping into the unknown, but often God uses it to bring healing to our souls.

The Bible uses the phrase "fear not" or "do not be afraid" 365 times: once for every day of the year. Unhealthy fear paralyzes us, leaving us stuck in our struggles. We must be courageous. Courage is not the absence of fear. It is not being without doubt or uncertainty regarding a situation. Courage is understanding the difficulty and challenges of a situation and choosing to face it anyway. When you are no longer running from the pain that brought you to your struggle or the pain that living in your struggle caused, that is when healing begins. Now you are ready to face it head-on with the help of others and with the help of God. You must be true to yourself and face your deepest darkest pains to find healing. Moving aside the fear of judgment, the fear of failure, the fear of nothing changing, take courage and trust that God's grace is sufficient, that there is no failure in soul seeking, and that God has the power to change you from the inside out.

"Be strong and courageous. Do not be afraid or terrified because of them, for the LORD your God goes with you; he will never leave you nor forsake you." (Deuteronomy 31:6)

"Have I not commanded you? 'Be strong and courageous. Do not be afraid; do not be discouraged, for the LORD your God will be with you wherever you go." (Joshua 1:9)

"For God has not given us a spirit of fear, but of power and of love and of a sound mind." (2 Timothy 1:7 NKJV)

God is with us. He does not place fear from our past in our hearts. Instead, He gives us the courage to face our past, to recognize our fears, and to overcome them. Self-reliance will fail us and keep us from healing. God-reliance propels us forward. Pray and ask God to give you the courage to take an honest look at your fears.

———

Make a list of who or what you fear and why? Be specific. (It's okay to have fear; it's not okay to hide it.) _____

_____

_____

_____

How do you respond destructively or negatively to your fears?

_____

_____

_____

How have your fears affected your friendships, your family, your work, and your romantic relationships?

_____

_____

_____

5
FINDING THE PAIN

MANdentity men reject passivity.

*"Do not merely listen to the word, and so deceive yourselves.
Do what it says." (James 1:22)*

MANdentity men honestly admit their resentments, fears, wrongs, and pain. What do we do when our back is against the wall? How do we respond in a moment of crisis? I've always heard that if you back a dog into a corner, he will fight. Meaning, everyone has a breaking point, everyone has a line if crossed will cause them to lash out. King Hezekiah, a leader of God's people, was backed into a corner by the Assyrian empire. The Assyrians were known for their brutal treatment of kings and communities who resisted them. Facing incredible danger, almost certain death, and the destruction of his kingdom, Hezekiah taught all of us a lesson. It's a lesson when implemented provides healing and hope for the believer.

> Hezekiah received the letter from the messengers and read it. Then he went up to the temple of the Lord and spread it out before the Lord. And Hezekiah prayed to the Lord: "Lord, the God of Israel, enthroned between the cherubim, you alone are God over all the kingdoms of the earth. You have made heaven and earth. Give ear, Lord, and hear; open your eyes, Lord, and see; listen to the words

Sennacherib has sent to ridicule the living God. It is true, Lord, that the Assyrian kings have laid waste these nations and their lands. They have thrown their gods into the fire and destroyed them, for they were not gods but only wood and stone, fashioned by human hands. Now, Lord our God, deliver us from his hand, so that all the kingdoms of the earth may know that you alone, Lord, are God." (2 Kings 19:14-19)

How did Hezekiah respond when his back was against the wall? He took everything to God in written form. This is the moment you get to unleash everything to a God who is fully capable of empathizing with you, as well as a God who has the power to heal you and the grace to forgive you. How do we heal? We must go back to the harm that we have caused others, the wrongs we have made and the same things that have been done to us. It's a journey through the valleys of the shadows of death, but we must remember God is with us. Healing and freedom await us at the end. In the columns below list every resentment and harm that you have caused or that you have towards another. God is with you and so are my prayers.

1. Schedule a day and time to begin.
2. Tell a trusted friend of your intentions and ask them to hold you accountable to complete it.
3. Find a quiet place to write.
4. Text or call your friend before you start and call or text when you finish.
5. Ask God to help you be completely honest and to give you the courage to hold nothing back.
6. Write down your resentments, fears, and pain. Be completely honest as you will use these finding the pain columns in the rest of this book.

Now you're ready!

FINDING THE PAIN

I'm Resentful Toward/I harmed/Harmed Me (people, institutions, situations)	The Cause (what specifically happened)	The Damage Affects My (self-esteem, security, ambitions, relationships, intimacy)

(Copy this page for personal use only and make as many copies of this section as needed to complete this lesson.)

That night the angel of the Lord went out and put to death a hundred and eighty-five thousand in the Assyrian camp. When the people got up the next morning—there were all the dead bodies! So Sennacherib king of Assyria broke camp and withdrew. He returned to Nineveh and stayed there. (2 Kings 19:35-36)

———

For the LORD your God is the one who goes with you to fight for you against your enemies to give you victory. (Deuteronomy 20:4)

6
CONFESSION

When I try to picture my father's face, all I can see is the picture in his obituary in the local newspaper. Trying to picture my father's face takes my thoughts back to the broken and lost nineteen-year-old I once was. At nineteen I was laying on a dungy old brown couch in a rundown one-bedroom apartment. The alcoholic manager and violence of the area advanced my application quickly there. It was the first place I had stayed since living in my car for the previous year. Thanksgiving, Christmas, and the New Year passed with me alone on the old couch smoking weed and sipping beers. One night while on my back staring at the ceiling I shook my fist towards heaven mumbling these words through tears, "Why won't you help me? Help me please." That was seventeen years ago, I'm thirty-six now with a pretty good memory and yet I can barely picture my father's face. In my mind I catch flashes of him smiling right after sipping a bottle of Budweiser. He's been dead for only five years, but it seems like an eternity.

I'm certain the reason I have a hard time remembering my father as I reflect on the past is because I feel like he never really saw me. I was just another one of his aggrevations—something else he was responsible for but did not necessarily enjoy.

What I do remember is him laughing while drinking with his friends, but not so much with me or our family. I rarely saw him joyful when spending time with our little family. At times it felt like we were a burden to my father, like another piece of equipment in his construction business that he had to deal with. I can remember the anxiety I felt when his truck tires pulled into the red rock driveway at our home. I can feel the giant void of fatherly love I never received and the shame of his hurtful teasing directed at me in front of his friends and our family. Even the word "father," makes me anxious as I think about my kids and what I hope and pray they feel towards me. Maybe you can relate to the anxiousness of my pain.

It's such a lonely place in my soul, even decades later when I think of my relationship with my father. My mind wanders to the feeling of uneasiness I have around men I love and respect. I constantly have to fight the urges to prove myself, that I measure up, that I matter, that I'm good enough just being me. This is a by-product of feeling like I never measured up, like I never mattered, like I wasn't good enough for my own father to love me. I now understand our relationship failure was not my fault. The game was rigged against me. There was no way for me to win at having a good relationship with my father. I felt I wasn't good enough when in reality my father was emotionally and spiritual sick; he was an alcoholic. His connection to himself, God, and those around him was broken.

At the age of thirty, one night after preaching, I met my father and his wife for dinner. I remember he looked at me while sipping his bottle of Budweiser and with a more serious and scared look he said, "I'm done after the surgery." That's at least how I want to remember it. We were eating dinner a few blocks from Vanderbilt Medical Center in Nashville, Tennessee. He was set to have surgery on his liver the next morning to remove a spot as a direct result of his cirrhosis. The truth is my father did not say that he was quitting. He sat their sipping his longneck Budweiser, and it was his wife who said those words. She had a profound faith in my father and a seemingly joyful countenance. She went on to mention that he was taking medication as he began to taper off his normal drinking regiment. My dad's drinking routine at that time consisted of him working for a few weeks on the railroad and then drinking nonstop at the bar until a day or two before he left to go back to work. When he wasn't at the bar, he was lying in his bed recovering from the side effects of his drinking. She brought him food because he felt too bad to get up. His already damaged liver was taking a beating from his binges. That night my father and I sat close at the table, but we could not have been any farther apart.

My father was a redneck of sorts. He still was working with a dozer, frequently hunted and fished, wore camouflage, sported cowboy boots to work, and spent every waking moment drinking.

He could be harsh and violent but also gentle and kind; he was unpredictable and often a ticking time bomb. The final years of his life were spent in a town known for its racism and is avoided by people of color. He was a country boy who was raised on racial lies. It was embedded in his thinking but expressed only in private. My father loved country living. He lived by a beautiful lake full of fish and near rolling hills and forests with lots of wildlife. There was plenty of country to explore; it was a paradise for him. I spent most of my early years running around the same places as my father, enjoying the lake and partying like he did.

It was the late nineties when my father's drinking got out of control. He became violent and absent, eventually leaving my mom, and me at home to fend for ourselves while my brother was away at college. I turned to the culture for guidance. Gangster rappers and the men in gangster movies became my role models. Decades later, while sitting across from my father at dinner that night, I deeply longed to bridge the gap between us. But I also knew that we can change only ourselves, not other people.

There we were, my father the alcoholic redneck backhoe and dozer operator starring across the table at his son, who had gone from being arrested for trafficking cocaine to having an encounter with Jesus and was now pastoring an urban ministry. I had been clean and sober for five years at the time, was married to a black woman with biracial children, and was living in the big city. We were worlds apart.

Eight days after that meal, I sat in a hospital room weeping after making the decision to take my father off life support. The next day he passed away. His liver just was not strong enough to handle the surgery. His wife was right, that Budweiser had been his last beer. It is comforting to know that in the last few years of my father's life, we both said, "I love you," before hanging up. We both loved as best we could.

CONFESSION

MANdentity men regularly confess sin.

"Therefore confess your sins to each other and pray for each other so that you may be healed. The prayer of a righteous person is powerful and effective." (James 5:16)

We all laugh at the story of the toddler who gets caught with chocolate smeared across his lips. When his parents ask if he took a cookie from the jar, he emphatically responds, "Oh, no, no, no, I did not eat any cookies." It's humorous because the sweet toddler doesn't really understand right and wrong. Over and over again the toddler gets caught with his hand in the cookie jar and the patient mother chuckles at the innocence of her son. For us men, repeating the same mistakes over and over again just isn't funny anymore. We shouldn't be struggling with the same things we struggled with five, ten, or twenty years ago. The only way to break the cycle is to confess to God and someone else the exact natures of our wrongs, but most men do not enjoy sharing their struggles or past mistakes. In fact, most of us don't want to hear about other people's own personal struggles or mistakes much less for us to share our own. MANdentity men lay it all out in the open before God and someone we trust. In my journey to healing and true MANdentity, sharing my struggles has been one of the most powerful and transformative tools available.

"Confess your sins to one another and pray for one another, so that you may be healed." (James 5:16)

The Greek word used for "confess" is *exomologeo,* which means to fully agree and to acknowledge. When we willingly acknowledge and fully agree with our past mistakes and pains, it releases the stronghold of guilt, shame, and fear. We are no longer held captive by them. The very act of confession unlocks the grip sin has on our lives and then healing can take place.

Most of us have heard the story of how to catch a monkey in the wild. This story has been told in many different ways, but the lesson is always the same. Across several different continents people groups have developed a method for trapping monkeys.

Normally what happens is they take a coconut or a similar shaped object and drill a hole just large enough for a monkey's hand to get inside. They add some extra weight to the object, then put a piece of fruit inside and place it where a monkey will find it.

The monkey flattens his hand through the hole to get the food, but with the fruit in its grasp, the monkey cannot get its hand back out. The hole is too small for the monkey's hand to get out of when he chooses to hold onto the fruit, and the object is too heavy for the monkey to carry. Because the monkey will not let go, it becomes trapped. The animal gives up its freedom to hold on to a small piece of food. It's obvious that all the monkey needs to do is let go and it can escape. But because the monkey is not willing to let go, the monkey is trapped and eventually captured.

Just like the monkey, for MANdentity men, it's time to let it go. When we let go and share with another person, it frees us. This opens our hearts to be filled with the truth of Scripture. Many of us are so full of guilt, shame, and resentment that the peace of God's word cannot infiltrate our soul. One of the best things we can do for our soul is to confess our sin and the sin that has been done to us.

"If we confess our sins, he is faithful and just to forgive us our sins and to cleanse us from all unrighteousness."
(1 John 1:9)

"I acknowledged my sin to you, and I did not cover my iniquity; I said, 'I will confess my transgressions to the LORD,' and you forgave the iniquity of my sin. Selah" (Psalm 32:5 ESV)

"Whoever conceals their sins does not prosper, but the one who confesses and renounces them finds mercy." (Proverbs 28:13)

List the things you are hesitant to share with a trusted person and why you are questioning sharing it. _____

_____

_____

_____

What in your past do you feel guilty about? _____

_____

_____

_____

_____

"Therefore, there is now no condemnation for those in Christ Jesus." (Romans 8:1)

I sat in a small concrete room in downtown Nashville across from a spiritual advisor in my life, staring down at the columns from the finding the pain in chapter 5 containing all the pain of my past. It was nerve racking to say the least. The room felt like it was a thousand degrees! My words came between short breaths as anxiety pumped through my body. The person I had chosen to share my struggles with very calmly said, "Adam, let's pray." We prayed and then he sat quietly as I began to read what I had written down. From time to time he would interject to share his experience with the same issue, to affirm a feeling, or give me a different perspective on how things were or show me patterns of behavior. The temperature in the room began to drop, my breathing slowed to normal, and a peace began to flow through my body. Every time I've shared a struggle of mine since then the same thing happens. I feel emotionally and spiritually better.

God has given us a powerful tool in our own healing process. We must let go of our fears of what the person with whom we are sharing will think. Often our guilt, shame, and pride prevents us from confessing our sin to a trusted friend. The voice of Satan ("the accuser" in Hebrew) will try to fill our heads and hearts with fear. He doesn't want us to confess our mistakes. God tells us that "He gave us a spirit not of fear but of power and love and self-control" (2 Timothy 1:7 ESV). God is not discouraging you from sharing your finding the pain columns with a trusted friend. Satan is. This is a moment as a MANdentity man in which we must courageously lead.

What struggles or unhealthy behaviors have you repeated over and over again? _____

_____

_____

_____

_____

_____

      I've heard it said that time heals all wounds. This is not true. Does time take away the pressure? Yes. But it does not remove the pain underneath the surface. It does not get to the root of the hurt, the resentment, the guilt. Time pushes the pain down deep until something triggers it. Think of a wound without a bandage that brushes against a rough surface. We feel the wound much more intensely when something touches it. This is especially true in our relationships. There is often a trail of damaged relationships when we look back over our past. We begin the process of rebuilding those relationships and healing when we confess. God already knows what happened, and He has sent someone to encourage you through the wreckage of your past. I can assure you that you will know a new freedom, a new peace, and a new happiness after sharing the resentments and pain from the columns in finding the pain from chapter five with another person.

One of the hardest things to do when moving toward healing is to face your true self. Most of us don't mind telling another person our strengths or even the wrong things others have done to us. But exposing our struggles is like the sound of nails on a chalkboard. We avoid it at all costs. In order to experience healing and overcome, you have to expose your sin. It's important to remember there is no judgment in confessing your struggles, and it is most definitely not a competition of who has done the most wrong. Anything that you hide in your heart and do not share is a bridge to your past struggles though. It leaves a dark hidden bridge back to your old ways. You must not leave anything out. You must bare your soul to another person to be free from the pain and wreckage and guilt of your past. Share everything you wrote down in the columns in chapter 5 with a trusted friend or counselor, and your pain and struggle will lose its control over you. You can't tell half-truths or confess only part of the struggles. Rather complete honesty is the key to spiritual and emotional healing.

———

When you heard about Christ and were taught in Him in accordance with the truth that is in Jesus. You were taught, with regard to your former way of life, to put off your old self, which is being corrupted by its deceitful desires; to be made new in the attitude of your minds; and to put on the new self, created to be like God in true righteousness and holiness. (Ephesians 4:21-24)

Confession is a cleansing process and an empowering moment in our journey to healing. We are essentially exposing our wounds, and in turn God heals them. This is how you gain balance and centeredness. When you confess your struggles, you are free to begin groundbreaking and revolutionary kingdom building. God gives you a clean slate, and you will be amazed at what He will do with your life.

Why has it been so difficult to trust others in your past? Be specific

_____

_____

_____

_____

_____

Why is trust so important in taking the spiritual action of confession?

_____

_____

_____

_____

List three people you trust today and why you trust them. _____

_____

_____

_____

_____

Choose one of the three people you listed above to share your finding the pain columns with. _____

_____

_____

_____

Healing literally means to make whole. I had so much brokenness that being broken felt normal. The process of healing sometimes is unsettling and can feel counter-productive. Just as a good home requires a strong foundation, getting healthy requires a strong foundation. The foundation of getting healthy is letting go of your secrets. I've heard it said that we are only as sick as our secrets. Victory over your struggle is right around the corner. Don't quit before the miracle happens and don't quit after it happens either. So many have stopped at this point and have unfortunately fallen back into their struggle.

Do you have any specific fears about sharing your resentments and painful moments with another person? _____

_____

_____

_____

_____

Is there anything you're still holding onto, something that you did not write on the chart in chapter 5? Why? _____

_____

_____

_____

_____

_____

What time and what day will you share your resentments and painful moments with your trusted friend, spiritual advisor, or counselor?_____

_____

_____

_____

_____

Our struggles have brought brokenness or because of brokenness we have struggled. We've began learning how it happened and now it's time to release it all. It's important to remember that God heals us eternally when we receive His son, but He gives us each other to heal daily from our earthly pains through confession. Please trust this process. Take courage and use the little bit of willingness you have to confess. Before moving to chapter 7, confess to God and share with a trusted man everything you wrote in your finding the pain columns in chapter 5.

7
DISCOVERING HOW TO FEEL

My uncle Kenny and I stood on the front porch of my child-hood home, a double-wide trailer tucked away in the woods. "I just want a family," I sobbed. Standing in silence except for my snif-fling. I said it again, but a little louder. "I just want a family." We were both drunk and we've never spoken about it since, but for the only time in my life my uncle said something that was not crazy. "You will. You will. You will have your own one day," he said. I hadn't seen or spoken to my dad in at least a year, but one of his friends was inside smoking amphetamines with my brother, my pill addicted mom was never around, and I was standing on the porch with my uncle, both drunk as a skunk. The hope of a future family faded fast.

My uncle had spent the last twenty years on the run from a child support debt. Never obtaining a driver's license or putting an-ything in his name simple to elude his legal responsibility of being a dad. But for the past week, he had been a friend. He had planned to come spend a week with us the summer after I graduated high school. Uncle Kenny found out quickly that I was the only one around. My mom came by once and my brother showed up late that particular night to do drugs. Maybe that's why he chose to come outside and stand on the porch with me. Even an alcoholic deadbeat dad could see that I had no one. Just moments before I had threatened my brother if he chose to use amphetamines. He looked at me with no emotion and black eyes and said, "let's go." I turned not out of fear but out of disgust.

This was my life; my entire family had chosen drugs and alcohol over us. That's when I stepped out onto the porch and stood stoically in a silent emptiness that I would not wish on my worst enemy. The former star athlete was now drunk and a druggy, blaming myself for all the pain in my life. Why did I keep quitting the sports I loved in the middle of the season? Why did I keep hurting the one person that cared about me and supported me, my girlfriend? Why couldn't I stop using and just focus on education, sports, and friends like all the other high-schoolers? If only I could go back to that moment and say to myself, "Adam, it's not your fault. Your family is sick right now, but one day they will get better. Love yourself. You are a great kid." I realize now that in my healing process I can speak directly to that eighteen-year-old kid. I felt so alone. I can say, "You are not alone." I felt unwanted. I can say, "You are wanted. You are worth it." I felt helpless. I can say, "There is so much hope and help for you."

Men are taught to tell our stories void of emotions. That's why the fish keeps getting bigger or the number of touchdowns keeps growing over the years in their stories. It's more about what happened instead of how we felt while it was happening. Living out our God given MANdentity means to fully connect emotionally with our past and present. I've spent years listening to men weep on the phone as their lives were falling apart. I've spent years talking with men so frustrated at themselves for acting out of character. I've spent years counseling men living their life totally detached emotionally and spiritually from the ones they love most. I've spent years journaling, working through recovery tools, participating in counseling and group therapy and leading counseling sessions and group counseling sessions. I've learned to connect feelings with events. This chapter provides you with the tools to begin this journey. I promise if you honestly use them, there will be depth and understanding that will allow you to learn how to love yourself and others better. It takes time and practice, but so does anything worth having. The connection point starts now as you discover how to feel.

DISCOVERING HOW TO FEEL

MANdentity men express how they feel in a healthy way.

"And after you have suffered a little while, the God of all grace, who has called you to his eternal glory in Christ, will himself restore, confirm, strengthen, and establish you."
(1 Peter 5:10 ESV)

One of the *joys* of finding healing and freedom from working through the MANdentity book is that MANdentity men get their feelings back. At the same time one of the *pains* of finding healing and freedom from working through the MANdentity book is that MANdentity men get their feelings back! I'll never forget the first meeting with my probation officer. My wife and I had just decided it would be best if I stayed home to babysit our two boys while she continued her job. They were both toddlers and the cost of two kids in daycare was almost equal to the pay of any job I could get at that time. My probation officer didn't take kindly to the news and in a firm voice and with a wagging finger she informed me I better have a job the next time she met with me. The energy in my body slowly faded like a balloon with a small hole, and an emotional fog filled my mind. On my drive home I felt depressed and anxious, so I called my mentor. After explaining the situation, he gave a slight chuckle and said, "sounds like your disappointed not depressed."

> "The heart is deceitful above all things and beyond cure. Who can understand it?" (Jeremiah 17:9)

Emotional and spiritual healing happens when we match our feelings with our experiences and connect them with our patterns of thinking and behaving. Most of us have not taken a Bible class or even participated in a Bible study that connected the feelings of Bible characters and the stories of their lives. Yet most of us have experienced painful situations and feelings in our lives much like the biblical characters we study in Scripture. When we lack biblical truth and emotional understanding, two things normally happen to us men when we experience painful events. One is that we separate our feelings from our experiences. We disassociate ourselves from the painful feelings we experienced during traumatic events in our lives. Two, that pain continues to live beneath the surface and tends to unexpectedly spew out.

Jeremiah teaches us that we cannot always trust our feelings. As we overcome our struggles, we must connect our feelings to the truth. I'm not saying that what you felt was a lie, because how you felt is how you felt. What I am saying is this: feeling something about yourself because you misinterpreted a situation or you stuffed the feelings you had during a situation that took place in your life is harmful. Emotionally misinterpreting situations in our lives creates a false sense of self. The product of a false interpretation of who we are is a broken identity. This leads us to seek security and contentment in sinful struggles. But God wired our MANdentity in the truth of how we feel in painful moments in our lives. When we hold onto false feelings about our identity because we never actually took the time to understand the truth about our difficult situations we've faced, we go around living in a LIEdentity instead of a MANdentity.

> "He was a murderer from the beginning, not holding to the truth, for there is no truth in him. When he lies, he speaks his native language, for he is a liar and the father of lies." (John 8:44)

One of Satan's tricks is to get us to believe a lie about who we are based on the lie of our past feelings. These false narratives are normally built from harmful situations or interactions with the adults in our lives. For instance, when I was a teenager living with my mom, she pulled a muscle in her back that gave her doctor the green light to prescribed prescription narcotics. Soon my highly educated and loving mother was consuming large amounts of narcotics. Her addiction wreaked havoc on both of our lives. My supportive mother was replaced with a depressed, emotionally unstable, and dangerously addicted mother. As her problems began to pile up, the pressure on me to keep her alive rose. Soon I was fighting a winless battle. She grew more and more addicted, more and more unhealthy, more and more broken, and I began to feel less and less of a man. Why? Because I started to believe emotional lies about this challenging situation.

Why can't I fix her? I thought. *I'm not good* enough to fix her. Why won't she just stop for me? I'm not good enough for her to stop for me. The father of lies began to whisper these lies and I internalized all the feelings that came with them. I hurt myself and others for years believing that I was not good enough. This was a lie from Satan embedded in my thoughts and in my LIEdentity. Today I know that it was not me and that as a kid and teen I was most certainly worthy of love and support from a healthy mother. "Do not conform to the pattern of this world, but be transformed by the renewing of your mind. Then you will be able to test and approve what God's will is—his good, pleasing and perfect will" (Romans 12:2). Going back and seeking to understand how we felt emotionally during the difficult moments in our lives is a part of renewing our minds to Gods true MANdentity for each of us. I am good enough, but Satan has tried to prevent me for years from uncovering this truth. Many men have years of emotional pain built on the lies of Satan. Voices of those who've harmed us echo in our soul and push us toward those lies. Our deceitful hearts have led us astray emotionally.

Let's journey through what you wrote in the columns of Finding the Pain in chapter 5 and find your true feelings within your experiences. With the help of your mentor, it's time to replace the lies Satan has told you with the truth. Below is a list of feelings to help you put words to what you felt.

MANdentity Feelings List

I feel **happy.** Here is a list of different happy feelings:

Aroused	Hopeful	Optimistic
Accepted	Inspired	Respected
Cheeky	Inquisitive	Sensitive
Confident	Joyful	Successful
Content	Loving	Thankful
Courageous	Peaceful	Trusting
Creative	Playful	Valued
Curious	Powerful	
Free	Proud	

I feel **surprised.** Here is a list of different surprised feelings:

Amazed	Disillusioned	Excited
Astonished	Dismayed	Perplexed
Awe	Eager	Shocked
Confused	Energetic	Startled

I feel **bad.** Here is a list of different bad feelings:

Apathetic	Out of Control	Sleepy
Bored	Overwhelmed	Stressed
Busy	Pressured	Tired
Indifferent	Rushed	Unfocused

I feel fearful. Here is a list of different fearful feelings:

Anxious	Inferior	Rejected
Excluded	Insecure	Scared
Exposed	Insignificant	Threatened
Frightened	Nervous	Weak
Helpless	Overwhelmed	Worried
Inadequate	Persecuted	Worthless

I feel angry. Here is a list of different angry feelings:

Aggressive	Furious	Provoked
Annoyed	Hostile	Resentful
Betrayed	Humiliated	Ridiculed
Bitter	Indignant	Skeptical
Critical	Infuriated	Violated
Dismissive	Jealous	Withdrawn
Distant	Let Down	
Frustrated	Mad	

I feel disgusted. Here is a list of different disgusted feelings:

Appalled	Disappointed	Judgmental
Awful	Embarrassed	Nauseated
Detestable	Hesitant	Repelled
Disapproved	Horrified	Revolted

I feel **sad.** Here is a list of different sad feelings:

Abandoned	Empty	Isolated
Ashamed	Fragile	Lonely
Depressed	Grief	Powerless
Despair	Guilty	Remorseful
Disappointed	Hurt	Victimized
Embarrassed	Inferior	Vulnerable

FEELING EXERCISE

Read back over your columns of Finding the Pain in chapter 5. Try to connect the specific emotions you felt during each situation that you listed. Answer the questions below for each situation as you move through them. Feel free to reference the feelings chart during this section of the book. Close your eyes and ask God to allow you to feel these feelings and to give you truth statements to guard your heart against any lies Satan may have told you. It is very important during these exercises that you are keenly aware of what your body is saying: the sensations you have, the rising of your breath, the pounding of your heart, and the feeling in your gut all have a story to tell. Now is the time to start listening. For so long we have walked around detached emotionally and spiritually from what are bodies are trying to tell us. Many of us are disconnected from the actual pain we felt during traumatic and hurtful moments in our lives. We say things and do things without feeling or regard for the feelings of those around us. This is how the lies pile up and how we become detached from everyone and everything. I have shared one from my life as an example.

I felt these feeling during this situation or toward this person.

While this was happening, I felt...

When my mom was using drugs and putting her addiction above caring for me, I felt unloved, angry, confused, and insecure. When I would come home to an empty house, I felt scared, abandoned, and unwanted. It was confusing when she would say she loved me, but her actions were so selfish and self-absorbed.

After this happened, I felt...

I felt like my choices didn't really matter. Nothing I did mattered because my own mother didn't see the value in caring for me. I started using people, places, and things for my own benefit without any regard for their feelings. Even when I cared for them at some point what I wanted overshadowed any reasoning of thinking of the feelings of another. I stopped believing people truly loved me.

Never trusting genuine love, support, and concern from others. I stopped loving myself.

I now know the truth is…

I now know I was deserving of love, attention, and support. I was a good kid who deserved a loving mother. Because of this truth I am willing to learn healthy ways to love, support, and care for others. I enjoy healthy attachments in the relationships that I have. I am fully capable of being loved and offering love in a healthy capacity. If and when I need help in this area, I am not afraid to ask for help or clarity on something that I don't understand. And today, I love myself.

I felt these feeling during this situation or toward this person.

While this was happening, I felt...

_____

_____

_____

_____

After is happened, I felt...

_____

_____

_____

_____

I now know the truth is... (ask your mentor for help if you need it)

_____

_____

_____

_____

I felt these feeling during this situation or toward this person.

While this was happening, I felt...

_____

_____

_____

_____

After is happened, I felt...

_____

_____

_____

_____

I now know the truth is... (ask your mentor for help if you need it)

_____

_____

_____

_____

I felt these feeling during this situation or toward this person.

While this was happening, I felt…

_____

_____

_____

_____

After is happened, I felt…

_____

_____

_____

_____

I now know the truth is… (ask your mentor for help if you need it)

_____

_____

_____

_____

I felt these feeling during this situation or toward this person.

While this was happening, I felt...

_____

_____

_____

_____

After is happened, I felt...

_____

_____

_____

_____

I now know the truth is... (ask your mentor for help if you need it)

_____

_____

_____

_____

I felt these feeling during this situation or toward this person.

While this was happening, I felt...

_____

_____

_____

_____

After is happened, I felt...

_____

_____

_____

_____

I now know the truth is... (ask your mentor for help if you need it)

_____

_____

_____

_____

I felt these feeling during this situation or toward this person.

While this was happening, I felt…

_____

_____

_____

_____

After is happened, I felt…

_____

_____

_____

_____

I now know the truth is… (ask your mentor for help if you need it)

_____

_____

_____

_____

(Copy this page for personal use only and make as many copies of this section
as needed to complete this lesson.)

After completing this exercise, go over what you wrote with your mentor. Allow them to help you attach biblical truth to the feelings of your past and how you can live in that truth today.

"Then you will know the truth, and the truth will set you free." (John 8:32)

My prayer is that this lesson will help set you free from the emotional lies that have kept you captive. It also is a tool to strengthen the accountability with your mentor and with others. Now you know the lies Satan has told you and will continue to try and tell you. With the help of Scripture, accountability partners, and your mentor, you can choose to live in the truth of your past instead of the lies.

"Where no counsel is, the people fall: but in the multitude of counselors there is safety." (Proverbs 11:14 KJV)

8
IDENTIFYING OUR CHARACTER

Healing sometimes comes quickly and sometimes slowly. Change is the same way. I went from sitting in a cell and then a treatment facility to living with my wife, two-year-old and three-month-old baby in a flash. I was grateful to be there for my family, but I found it hard to change my character. Each day the pressure would build in my head and in my heart. I spent so much energy toward doing the right thing and not enough energy toward becoming the right person. Cooking dinner, caring for my boys, and doing my best to be good for my wife was noble, but changing inwardly brings real change.

The interactions with my family were like watching Jim Carrey's character Stanley Ipkiss transform from a shy bank clerk into a reality-bending trickster in his hit movie *The Mask*. In the movie Stanley Ipkiss finds an ancient mask that when placed over his face turns him into a totally different person. He is transformed into a mischievous reflection of himself, after the first night of wearing the mask Stanley wakes up and says, "It's everything I always wanted to be but never had the courage to become." He soon realizes the person he becomes while wearing the mask is a far cry from who he truly is and from who he wants to become. Like Stanley Ipkiss, I wore a mask and did what I thought a good man would do while stuffing all my true feelings. Hiding my true feelings behind the mask of good deeds. Eventually I started having little explosions. One day I got upset and broke one of the chairs to my kids' *Cars* table set. Thank the Lord my kids weren't around at that moment. After calming down I was embarrassed and confused, "How could I do such a thing?" That's when I realized what I don't talk out constructively I will act out destructively. Instead of wearing a good man mask for the world, I realized it was better for me to show my true face and express what I'm feeling. I must admit, it's embarrassing and at times humiliating to "grow up" in front of other adults. But that is exactly what I needed. God wants to transform the real me, not the masked me.

After praying and thinking about what I had done, I thought maybe I could fix the chair, but it was hopeless. I quickly grabbed the broken chair and threw it in the trash, attempting to hide the destruction I caused because I couldn't fix it myself. This was how I had reacted to all of my struggles in the past, but now I realized that was not a good solution. It only postpones the consequences and perpetuates the pain of my mistakes. It is up to us to address the negative and positive elements of our character. It is up to you to ask for help. On my way back inside after tossing the broken chair in the garbage my wife met me at the door. With a firm but kind tone she said, "You are not allowed to treat us how you feel. You are allowed to treat us like we deserve. You need to address whatever is happening with you."

I realized that I couldn't keep handling difficulty the way I had in the past. It was time to begin dealing with my character. From time to time I experienced moments like these where I wanted to change how I felt but could not express my emotional needs in healthy ways. Outburst of unhealthy emotion never helped. They only sounded an alarm that something inside of me, something in my character, needed to be addressed.

No one arrives at a destination without traveling there first. Simply idea, right? The same principle applies to the flaws and strengths in our character. We need to go back and determine how we arrived at where we currently are. How did I arrive at believing that yelling and breaking stuff was an appropriate method for handling stressful situations? After looking back over my columns of Finding the Pain in chapter 5, I realized that my father exhibited the same behavior and many of the characters in movies I grew up watching showed the same behavior as well. Once I learned how it started, I could begin to identify why and how to change the behavior. Then I started practicing those changes. Reading Scripture and talking to my mentor helped me with this process. It's a process that takes time and, in some instances, lots of failure. MANdentity men know that sometimes failure leads to success when we are failing in the direction of obedience. God's grace is sufficient for our mistakes. Our part is to keep on moving forward in the direction of obedience.

IDENTIFYING OUR CHARACTER

MANdentity men pursue Godly character.

"When I was a child, I spoke like a child, I thought like a child, I reasoned like a child. When I became a man, I gave up childish ways." (1 Corinthians 13:11 ESV)

Have you ever gotten all dressed up to go out with your friends only to have the first person you see point out a huge stain on your shirt? We have all had similar instances such as this. Moments where we thought we were looking our best or moments where we thought we had overcome something only to realize we had not. Moments when we think we are making progress only to realize we are just denying the disfunction in our lives or maybe we just can't see the stain on our shirt. Our attention has been focused on our past, how to heal from it and how to overcome it. Our behavior is directly connected to our past hurts and to the pain we have caused others. However, it is imperative in the transformation process that we address our character struggles now. Our true MANdentity depends on it.

> "For the grace of God has appeared, bringing salvation for all people, training us to renounce ungodliness and worldly passions, and to live self-controlled, upright, and godly lives in the present age, waiting for our blessed hope, the appearing of the glory of our great God and Savior Jesus Christ, who gave himself for us to redeem us from all lawlessness and to purify for himself a people for his own possession who are zealous for good works." (Titus 2:11-14 ESV)

Renouncing ungodliness and worldly passions so that we can live self-controlled, upright, and godly lives happens when we identify the unhealthy patterns in our life. Again, we need the help of God and others while searching our columns of Finding the Pain in chapter 5 for these defects of character. I'll never forget when my middle son, Joe Joe, was just a little over a year old. I came into the kitchen to see the refrigerator door cracked open. A plastic bowl was stuck in between the door and the shelves preventing the door from completely closing. A few minutes earlier I had cut an entire box of strawberries and placed them in the now empty bowl on the bottom drawer of the refrigerator. A trail of red juice was coming from the fridge onto the kitchen floor and down the hall toward the boys' room. "Joe! Joe!" I yelled. My little toddler came waddling in the kitchen like a penguin on the frozen tundra holding a Matchbox car. "Did you eat the strawberries?" He quickly shook his head side to side while sheepishly looking at me with his handsome brown eyes. "Are you suuuurrrrree, Joe? Joe?" I pressed. Again, his head shook while looking down this time. It was obvious that he was the culprit with the red juice stains on his little white t-shirt, the red juice dried on his mouth and hands. This is a sweet and funny memory for him and I. One in which we laugh about often, but this is also an insight into how without the proper guidance we can develop unhealthy patterns of behavior.

Sometimes we do not notice our unhealthy behaviors and even go as far as denying them when we are caught with juice stains on our shirt. In order to find healing from our bad behaviors, we must identify what they are. This is the type of self-awareness that brings long-term emotional and spiritual health and long-term healing from our struggle. When we humbly turn our struggles over to Jesus Christ, His grace is sufficient to forgive us and to help transform the behaviors that are affecting our character. If you do not address them now, eventually your old way of living will return and all the work you have done will be negated. Only a complete restart and slow trudging through your heart issues can bring lasting change. None of us want to go back, we want to keep moving forward. In order to keep moving forward you must uncover every rock and address every issue so that you can change not only how you feel about yourself and others but can begin actively living a life that is completely different than you have ever lived before—a life where your biblical identity is lived out. Your MANdentity! Below is a list of character defects and assets to help you identify the character you have exhibited.

> "But you also said that no matter how far away we were, we could turn to you and start obeying your laws. Then you would bring us back to the place where you have chosen to be worshiped." (Nehemiah 1:9 CEV)

Character Defects

Aimless	Apprehensive	Bored
Angry	Arrogant	Bothered
Anxious	Ashamed	Complacent

Confused	Inconsistent	Self-Condemnation
Controlling	Indifferent	Self-Indulgent
Covetous	Insecure/Shy	Self-Justification
Despondent	Insincere	Self-Pitying
Disappointed	Intolerant	Self-Righteous
Discontent	Irresponsible	Self-Seeking
Discourteous	Irritated	Selfish
Disgusted	Jealous	Silly
Dishonest	Judgmental	Slothful
Disrespectful	Lacking Discretion	Smug
Domineering	Lazy	Stubborn
Doubtful	Living in the Past	Suspicious
Envious	Lustful	Tense
Fearful	Out of Control	Ungrateful
Frightened	Overwhelmed	Unkind
Frustrated	Panicky	Unrealistic
Gluttonous	Pessimistic	Unreasonable
Greedy	Prideful	Unsafe
Grumpy	Procrastinating	Violent
Harmful	Gossip	Withdrawn
Hateful	Proud	Worrisome
Hyper	Resentful	Worthless
Impatient	Restless	
Inconsiderate	Self-Centered	

Character Assets

Accepting	Faithful	Present
Assertive	Forgiving	Prompt
Ambitious	Generous	Purposeful
Aware of Others	Gentle	Realistic
Calm	Happy	Reasonable
Careful	Helpful to Others	Relaxed
Caring	Honest	Responsible
Cheerful	Hopeful	Seeking Spiritual
Confident	Humble	Growth
Consistent	Industrious	Serene
Constructive	Kind	Sincere
Content	Living for Today	Stable
Cooperative	Loving	Thoughtful
Courteous	Open-minded	Tolerant
Discreet	Optimistic	Trusting
Empathetic	Outgoing	Trustworthy
Engaged	Patient	
Excited	Prayerful	

Please review your columns of Finding the Pain in chapter 5 and the MANdenity Feelings List. Once you have looked these over, please list your character flaws along with the reason why you see it as a flaw based on what you wrote in the columns in finding the pain, a sentence or two about how this behavior has contributed to your struggle, and a sentence or two about what patterns you have developed in your life as a result of this character flaw. There might be additional character flaws that you've noticed in your life present day. It's important to take every character struggle from our past and present through this exercise.

Character Flaw: _____

Why is this a character flaw for you? _____

_____

_____

_____

How has this behavior contributed to your current struggle? _____

_____

_____

_____

What patterns have you developed because of this character flaw? Or what bad behaviors have you continued to repeat because of this character flaw? _____

_____

_____

_____

Character Flaw: _____

Why is this a character flaw for you? _____

_____

_____

_____

_____

How has this behavior contributed to your current struggle? ____

_____

_____

_____

_____

What patterns have you developed because of this character flaw?
Or what bad behaviors have you continued to repeat because of
this character flaw? _____

_____

_____

_____

_____

Character Flaw: _____

Why is this a character flaw for you? _____

_____

_____

_____

_____

How has this behavior contributed to your current struggle? _____

_____

_____

_____

_____

What patterns have you developed because of this character flaw? Or what bad behaviors have you continued to repeat because of this character flaw? _____

_____

_____

_____

_____

Character Flaw: _____

Why is this a character flaw for you? _____

_____

_____

_____

_____

How has this behavior contributed to your current struggle? _____

_____

_____

_____

_____

What patterns have you developed because of this character flaw?
Or what bad behaviors have you continued to repeat because of
this character flaw? _____

_____

_____

_____

_____

Character Flaw: _____

Why is this a character flaw for you? _____

_____

_____

_____

_____

How has this behavior contributed to your current struggle? _____

_____

_____

_____

_____

What patterns have you developed because of this character flaw?
Or what bad behaviors have you continued to repeat because of
this character flaw? _____

_____

_____

_____

_____

Character Flaw: _____

Why is this a character flaw for you? _____

_____

_____

_____

_____

How has this behavior contributed to your current struggle? ____

_____

_____

_____

_____

What patterns have you developed because of this character flaw?
Or what bad behaviors have you continued to repeat because of
this character flaw? _____

_____

_____

_____

_____

Good Character Trait: _____

Why is this a character asset for you? _____

_____

_____

_____

_____

How has this behavior contributed to your current healing? _____

_____

_____

_____

_____

What patterns or healthy behaviors have you developed because of

this character asset? _____

_____

_____

_____

_____

Good Character Trait: _____

Why is this a character asset for you? _____

_____

_____

_____

_____

How has this behavior contributed to your current healing? _____

_____

_____

_____

_____

What patterns or healthy behaviors have you developed because of

this character asset? _____

_____

_____

_____

_____

Good Character Trait: _____

Why is this a character asset for you? _____

_____

_____

_____

_____

How has this behavior contributed to your current healing? _____

_____

_____

_____

_____

What patterns or healthy behaviors have you developed because of

this character asset? _____

_____

_____

_____

_____

> "Therefore, I urge you, brothers and sisters, in view of God's mercy, to offer your bodies as a living sacrifice, holy and pleasing to God—this is your true and proper worship. Do not conform to the pattern of this world, but be transformed by the renewing of your mind. Then you will be able to test and approve what God's will is—his good, pleasing and perfect will." (Romans 12:1-2)

Now you have a working list of character flaws that have caused you to conform to unhealthy patters of living emotionally and spiritually. I urge you to present these to God and your mentor. Pray to God asking for the power to overcome your character flaws. Ask God to help transform them by renewing your mind to what is right and by giving you the power to change your behavior. As a result, you will understand what His will is for you moving forward. It is important to remember that God does not condemn us for our mistakes. He loved us before we were born. There is nothing we can do to earn His love and nothing we can do to lose His love. He freely gives it to us. His desire is that we experience life to its fullest and be free from our old patterns of living. It's also important to share your character assets with your mentor. These are parts of your character that you get to build on.

How have you justified your character flaws in the past?

_____

_____

_____

_____

Has there been a time recently when you were able to stop from acting out a character flaw and choose a healthy character trait?

_____

_____

_____

_____

What character assets are you most grateful for today?

_____

_____

_____

_____

Share each of your character flaws with God in prayer and ask Him to remove them. Practice this each day.

_____

_____

_____

_____

_____

9
PRACTICING FORGIVENESS

My wife, two boys, and I went to visit my dad one weekend. I was pastoring and doing my best to juggle work and life. I had made it to the point in my MANdentity journey where making amends for my past mistakes was paramount. The people who had harmed me the most were my mom and dad. How could I make amends for things I did while trying to just survive the chaos of my childhood?

The columns of Finding the Pain in chapter 5 helped me see all the pain that my parents had caused me, and it also open the door to the part I had played. Still making amends just did not make sense to me. I was a teenager, they were the adults, why should I forgive them and try to make things right when they never have? I was comparing myself to them, but comparison is very dangerous in the healing process. I needed to focus on offering my amends and seeking forgiveness.

Making amends may take you much longer than it took me, and that is okay. What is not okay is to compare the pain caused to us and the pain we caused others and make amends only if you caused more pain. MANdentity men move toward forgiveness, making amends no matter what. I talked everything over with my mentor and with my wife. I did not have much to ask my father's forgiveness for, but I could not help but wonder what he would think. Obviously, he knows that he left me when I was still young, he was a drunk, violent and a bully.

My wife, kids, and I all piled into our grey little Mazda mini-van and took the two-hour drive to his home for a visit like we normally would, but this time I planned to make amends. My palms were sweaty, and I was super nervous about this visit. I must have gone over our conversation a thousand times in my head before arriving at his home. They greeted us as usual with smiles and hugs, ushering us to place our stuff upstairs and grab a plate. My dad loved to cook meat, and he often would make prime rib au jus when we came to visit. Dad was drinking beer in a cup. He and his wife drank often, and they continued to do that even when we visited, although my dad agreed not to smoke in the house or drink alcohol in bottles when we were there. Even to this day my children do not know that Grandpa Bob was drinking around them. This was progress for my dad. He was drinking and laughing and telling jokes while watching TV. He slowly leaned forward while putting his recliner in the upright position and grabbed his cigarettes to smoke outside on the back porch.

By this time he had graduated to his usual mixed drink since supper was over, and it was past five o'clock. I had only been clean and sober and living for Jesus for two years at that point. Most of my time was spent playing matchbox cars and exploring the woods with my boys. My wife and I were both working full-time, and I was attending school. Dad closed the door, and it was like a vacuum pulled all the sound behind him. My thoughts and anticipation silenced the chatter and sound from the TV in the room.

It was now or never. I stood up and slowly walked outside. I could feel each beat of my heart and hear each footstep like a cowboy boot on a concrete floor. The boys were toddlers then and followed me outside to run around on the deck. I can't remember the exact words that I said because that doesn't matter. I just opened my mouth and made amends for being rebellious, for hitting him when he attacked my brother, and for the times I was hurtful.

Dad had a cigarette in his left hand and a mixed drink in a small glass in his right hand. His jaw hit the deck when I asked for his forgiveness and told him I was wrong for doing those things. He didn't cry; he didn't even respond. He just looked at me with disbelief. It was silent for about a minute or two and then the door flung open as my stepmom yelled, "Bob!" Dad walked inside, and I floated inside right behind him feeling as light as a feather. My dad never apologized for anything he had done to me. Maybe he thought he didn't need too. Maybe he thought putting food on the table for fourteen years was good enough. Maybe he thought helping my wife and first-born son move when I went to jail covered all of his mistakes. I don't know, and I don't care. That was between him and God. As for me, my heart was free. I could freely love my dad and others without the stain of the pain I caused in the relationship we had. After making my amends, our relationship was closer than it ever had been. Later I overheard him tell my wife and his wife that I said something to him that he thought I would never say. I'm not exactly how, but I know it meant something special for him. I continued this healing process with the help of my mentor, through my writing, and by praying extensively about it. Now, I am free to love more deeply those who I care about without my painful actions toward my dad and others distorting my view. After working through this chapter so will you.

PRACTICING FORGIVENESS

MANdentity men ask for forgiveness and offer forgiveness.

"For if you forgive others their trespasses, your heavenly Father will also forgive you, but if you do not forgive others their trespasses, neither will your Father forgive your trespasses."
(Matthew 6:14-15 ESV)

One Thursday night I was driving on a two-lane country road with my friends. We were sporting our high school football jerseys and passing blunts around. I was going more than ninety miles per hour when a state trooper passed me going the other direction. He immediately hit his breaks to turn around. I had to make a split-second decision. Lifting my foot off the gas there was only two options: slam the gas or slam the break. I quickly punched the gas hoping to elude the trooper and make it safely back for our weekly team meal the night before Friday's big game. With the gas pedal to the floor I began swerving through the turns hoping to make the last turn before he could see, but just as we rounded the sharp curve my friend in the back seat said, "stop he got us. He saw our tail end before you made the corner. We are hit."

As I pulled over and still out of his line of sight, we threw everything illegal we could out the windows. We could hear the clatter of his boots stomping the pavement and his handcuffs bouncing as he approached. He had his hand on his gun; clearly he was not the least bit happy.

"Step out of the car, boy!" he commanded. He was noticeable upset, but for some reason he was trying to stay calm. "Do you know what you just did?" he asked. "I can have you shipped to a juvenile detention center right now!" he said through clenched teeth. "What position do you play?" he asked. The last question startled me. He then asked me what positions my friends played. I told him. He then looked down at his feet while shaking his head and breathing through his nostrils. He began to lecture me on who I was with, what I had done, and what the consequences would mean for the team and its supporters. Then he said, "I live on this road and better not ever catch you driving that fast again. Get back in the car and slow down." At that point his voice was very calm and sort of shaky. It was as if he could not believe what he was doing.

Calling the drug dogs, waiting while they towed my car, and being in the papers for sending the local high school football team to juvenile detention was not what he wanted. But that was his job. We all probably have stories about times we were given grace—just as we all probably have stories when we were harshly punished.

One of the important principles in MANdenity is learning to be gracious, to practice forgiveness. This involves placing our ego aside. Ego is good for confidence, achieving goals, and pushing oneself to achieve new heights. God weaved an ego into each man's DNA. This shapes our MANdentity and can be a good thing. It is not good, however, when it prevents us from addressing harm that we've caused or harm that has been inflicted on us. The truth is most men have lots of unforgiveness deep inside their souls. It hurts. Physical pain is easier for men to overcome than emotional pain. A part of society tells us that tough men are not emotional. It tells us that our MANdentity should not encompass emotional hurt and that we should brush those feelings and thoughts to the side. This type of coping is dangerous and only feeds our struggle. It builds large unhealthy strongholds in places that God designed to have healthy strongholds. Places where are ego knows when to be confident, understands how to practice humility, and seeks emotional health. We must push through feelings that tell us "this won't change anything" and address unforgiveness.

"He does not treat us as our sins deserve or repay us according to our iniquities. For as high as the heavens are above the earth, so great is his love for those who fear him; as far as the east is from the west, so far has he removed our transgressions from us." (Psalms 103:10-12)

"But he said to me, 'My grace is sufficient for you, for my power is made perfect in weakness.' Therefore, I will boast all the more gladly about my weaknesses, so that Christ's power may rest on me." (2 Corinthians 12:9)

God's sufficient grace is not built on us forgetting our past. God's sufficient grace is built on us taking ownership of it. While I was living in my struggle and trapped inside my own head with its distorted thoughts and feelings, I harmed people. Many of us can relate. We had lots of hurt that was coming out in ways that were painful for ourselves and others.

I remember being with family on Christmas day. My son was just one year old at the time, and we had just spent the day opening presents and eating too much food. As the sun went down I began to feel restless. I wanted to get out of there, so I picked a fight and drove away from everyone who truly loved me. Deep down all I really wanted was to be loved, but I was so damaged emotionally that I could not receive love or give love in healthy ways. I pulled into an empty nightclub parking lot. The guilt started flowing. Waking up the next day alone in our apartment away from my son, my wife, and a family that was now trying to love me was humiliating. I had messed up again, and this time the guilty feelings hit me faster than normal. "Why do I hurt everyone I love?" I cried out. I was detached and disconnected. I was broken emotionally.

Do you have any lingering resentments that you're holding onto that are preventing you from forgiving? _____

_____

_____

_____

"I do not understand what I do. For what I want to do I do not do, but what I hate I do. And if I do what I do not want to do, I agree that the law is good. As it is, it is no longer I myself who do it, but it is sin living in me." (Romans 7:15-17)

There was too much hurt on top of hurt for me to see my part in anything. After working through the first eight chapters of this book, you are ready to look at *your* part in the people *you* harmed. This can be one of the most freeing things that you ever do, or it can be one of the most volatile things you ever do. Our tongues can be a tool or a torch. They can bring life or death, blessings or cursings. A little match can start a forest fire and a small rudder can steer a massive ship. Our tongues can be both powerfully dangerous and transformative. We must be wise in how we approach forgiveness, making sure we are not pampering our own ego or selfishly freeing ourselves from the weight of a mistake at the expense of another.

How is it beneficial to your long-term healing to determine the exact nature of your wrongs? _____

_____

_____

_____

Why is it important that you are very clear about your responsibility in the harm you caused? _____

_____

_____

_____

> "Be kind to one another, tenderhearted, forgiving one another, as God in Christ forgave you." (Ephesians 4:32 ESV)

It's important that you be kind to yourself during this process by remembering that everyone makes mistakes and acknowledging that Jesus Christ forgives you. We have a responsibility to forgive ourselves. It's also important that you are kind in how you make amends for your wrongs. I strongly urge you not to seek forgiveness for the harm you caused without sharing your intentions with a trusted Christian mentor, counselor, or pastor. Sometimes our willingness to make things right can cloud our judgment, and we wind up causing harm rather than building a bridge to heal a wound. While making amends is about addressing our part in the wreckage of our past, it is also about the other person. It's not about their response but about being kind to them. Having said that, there may be some individuals we will never be able to make amends with personally. We can ask God for forgiveness, forgive ourselves, and choose to never repeat such actions. Sometimes the people we harmed may have moved on and be in a great place with someone else, and it would be wrong for us to approach them now. Again, this is just an example and may not fit every situation. And sometimes you may need to approach people in healthy relationships even though you have harmed them. This is why it's important to seek godly counsel when making amends.

Are there people to whom you need to make amends but approaching them could cause harm or bring up harm to their current life? Write each name and the situation. _____

_____

_____

_____

_____

_____

Why in some situations is just changing your behavior not sufficient to repair the damage you have caused?_____

_____

_____

_____

_____

_____

Do you have amends to make that are financial? If so, explain the situation. _____

_____

_____

_____

_____

> "And when you stand praying, if you hold any-
> thing against anyone, forgive them, so that your
> Father in heaven may forgive you your sins."
> (Mark 11:25)

Several years back I was preaching a message on Mark 11 to the youth I was pastoring. In trying to explain the principle of this passage, I brought several bags of luggage on stage. Grabbing the first bag I explained that anything we have not addressed in our heart we carry into our relationships. Unforgiveness is one bag. Resentments is another bag. I continued to pick up bag after bag: anger, unwillingness to offer amends, guilt. I attempted to walk around while holding onto all the bags of luggage, but it was a struggle. Eventually I fell flat on my face and the crowd erupted with laughter! After calming them down, I stared deeply into each person's eyes in the crowd, tears began to roll down my cheeks, and my lips began to quiver. "This was me for so long," I said. Having been in so many of their homes and seeing and hearing about their pain, I told them, "this is so many of you right now."

That is what it's like for us when we try to be in relationships with others while holding onto unforgiveness. We can't move; it's as if we are frozen. No one else can see the bags, but we can feel them. And they are heavy. We want to love, offer support, and express ourselves, but we can barely walk. It's because there is so much unforgiveness and so many amends to people we have harmed that has not been addressed.

If you're reading this, it's most likely because you have been hurt and you have caused hurt. Over time if you continue to constructively talk out the pain that was inflicted on you, you can heal. I have. Now is the time to clean up your soul. Caring for your soul can feel humiliating, but humiliation and humility are confusing for the person who is healing emotionally. Humbly making amends is holy and a far cry from humiliating, don't let those feelings discourage you. It's important as you make amends that you remind yourself that your forgiveness is built on the foundation of a loving God who willingly chose to forgive and love you first.

"We love because he first loved us." (1 John 4:19)

Look back over your columns in Finding the Pain in chapter 5. List the people you have harmed and to whom you need to offer amends. Then list the people who have harmed you and who you must forgive. Write a brief explanation of what happened. Make sure to go over this list with your mentor before offering amends and/or sharing your decision to forgive them.

I harmed/was harmed by	What happened?

Answer these questions after you have offered your amends.

Were there any amends that did not go well? Explain what hap-
pened._____

_____

_____

_____

Were there any amends that went really well? It's important to affirm when you are moving forward and when growth is happening.

_____

_____

_____

_____

_____

10
HEART CHECK

Riding to the police station in the back of a cop car with my hands cuffed behind my back. I looked out the window at the businesses and the football field where I played in high school. I had driven these streets many times before, taking a car full of kids to church, bribing them to listen to the message with McDonalds burgers. I had watched parades, coached basketball at the middle school, and mentored students. The shame I felt touched every part of my being. I could sense the bravado and initial rush of the arresting officer waning as he asked if I had ever been arrested before. "Not really," I replied softly. The arrogance and pride that I had become accustom to had left, and I felt defeated. The silence of the ride was heavy, and the process began.

As we drove into the barbwire fence area a twelve-foot gate opened and closed for the cop car. We made our way to another steel garage door that opened and closed. Once out the officer strip searched me and gave me a change of clothes. Then he led me to a cell with another known drug dealer. Perhaps the largest and most respected drug dealer (respected by the hustlers that is) in our city. He was loud, angry, and seemed to view the indictments against him as a travesty. It was as though he believed he were innocent, and we both absolutely new he was not. We talked for a few hours while he constantly beat on the cell door. Finally, he was moved out of the holding cell. I sat alone on a concrete floor with a toilet sink combo and a concrete rectangle slab for a bed on the opposite end of the wall. Since seventy-two indictments had been issued to various drug dealers across the city, and most of them already had been arrested, they only had adult 4x black-and-white stripes, and no more orange slippers for me. I'm about five nine and 180 pounds.

Shivering on the cold floor, I heard the steel door finally slide open. "Phone call," the officer said. After cuffing my ankles and hands and using a steel chain to connect them, the officer led me out into the hall. I shuffled my way to the phone, trying to keep my pants from falling down. On my way I thought *Who am I going to call?* The lady behind the steel desk handed me the phone that was used only for new arrivals' first call. She looked at me with tears in her eyes. *Maybe it's because I look so young,* I thought. Then I realized she looked sad because she could sense that I really had no one to call, and it broke her heart. At that moment everyone in my life was either a part of the lifestyle I was living, or they were trying to stay as far away from me as possible.

Then it hit me, I had never returned to my son's mother's place after dropping the keys for the landlord. At least I could call her and tell her what happened. Reluctantly, I picked up the phone after staring at it for a few minutes and dialed her number. She answered the phone, and I shared the news with her. There was a long pause on the other end, and I closed my eyes, tensing my entire body as I anticipated her judgment. It wasn't like she had ever really been mean or harsh to me. It was just that she had every right to let it all out. She had every right to tell me what a horrible man I had been and a horrible father I was to our son and the one on the way. (She was five months pregnant with our second son.) This was her moment to put me in my place and pay me back for all the pain and misery I had caused her. She said, "Adam, this is from God." Pausing for a second or two, she went on to tell me that God had a plan for my life and that she believed in me. For the next five minutes she gave me more hope than I had ever had in the first twenty-five years of my life. She believed in me when I did not believe in myself. As she was about to hang up the phone, I must have said something because I heard my one-and-half-year-old son say, "Daddy!". There was such joy in his voice. The tears rolled down my face and of the face of the receptionist. My son had yelled Daddy so loudly that both the receptionist and the officer heard it. We were all crying. This wonderful woman who is now my wife said, "I love you and I'm going to help you" before hanging up. All three of us wiped away the tears, and I shuffled back to my cell.

HEART CHECK

MANdentity men establish consistent accountability in their lives.

"Where no counsel is, the people fall: but in the multitude of counsellors there is safety." (Proverbs 11:14 KJV)

In the Psalms David opens himself up to God's inspection. In Psalm 139, David's request for a holy God to explore the depths of his soul is something each of us must pursue daily in order to live out a holy identity. David wants God not only to inspect his heart but to put him to the test with the desire that his life be transformed.

I've always enjoyed coaching my children's athletic teams. My wife tells me that sometimes it appears that I'm more excited about the games and practices than they are. Football is one of my favorite sports to coach and often brings in the largest number of athletes. The first day of football practice with a new team goes about the same each year. I put each athlete through a series of drills to test their agility, speed, strength, and catching and throwing abilities. It's how we inspect the gift sets of our players and how we learn their weaknesses. David is asking for God to do the same for him each day. "Put my heart and actions each day to your test

Lord," is the request that David makes. It's a healthy pattern of living for all men and affords us the opportunity to celebrate our wins and learn from our losses each day. MANdentity men develop a healthy pattern of allowing God to examine their hearts. This is not to condemn us, but rather to free us.

We have all seen the movies when two people turn to each other smiling and say, "Are you thinking what I'm thinking?" This is a fun, joyous moment between two people because it affirms that their hearts and spirits are aligned. We never have to ask God this question though, because He already knows our thoughts. Opening our hearts to God on a daily basis is not to inform Him, it's so He can transform us. Every believer in Jesus Christ has God's Spirit living in them. The rewarding thing about a daily inventory of our lives is that a gracious, merciful, loving, all-knowing, and kind God is the presiding Judge. In Him there's no condemnation. In fact, it's the exact opposite of condemnation.

> "So now there is no condemnation for those who belong to Christ Jesus." (Romans 8:1 NLT)

God desires to know our troubling thoughts and offensive ways so that He can lead us into victory through His grace and mercy. "Lead me in the way everlasting" is the cry for mercy from David to a loving God that possesses a never-ending well of grace and mercy for the believer. Our motivation is to continue living a life along biblical and Spirit-filled principles. This is a daily process of inspecting the good, the bad, and the ugly in your life. This is how we live out our true, God-designed MANdentity. We each surrender our strengths and weaknesses as the Spirit prompts us to adjust our actions and attitudes. In the same token, God's power is activated as we humbly acknowledge and surrender our weaknesses and as we celebrate our gifts.

Think about your last few weeks at work, school, home, or with family. What behaviors reflect something opposite of who you desire to become? Focus on your reactions (words and behaviors) to challenges, frustrations, and things that didn't go as planned.

_____

_____

_____

Examine yourselves to see whether you are in the faith; test yourselves." 2 Corinthians 13:5 "

Early in my marriage I found it easy to blame my wife for my own struggles. I also blamed the proverbial They and anyone else I could. One of the most important principles in our spiritual journey is to continue to take a daily inventory and when we are wrong quickly admit it.

After spending the first nineteen years of my life in the country, the last two decades of city life have been an eye-opener. One of the more comical things in living in suburban America for me has been the imaginary mow line. My wife and I have lived on these small plots of land with roughly twenty feet separating the homes adjacent to ours. Every time my neighbors mow their grass before me, they leave a line that separates their yard from mine. No one knows if its accurate, but once it has been established it is not to be crossed unless a city inspector comes out and places sticks that indicate official property lines. Things run smoothly if both parties sort of agree on this imaginary mow line, but the second either side crosses that line trouble comes. The idea here is to keep your side of the lawn clean and to stay away from the other side. Even if they are two weeks behind on their mowing, in the world of suburban America mow etiquette, you must never try and mow their side of the lawn. Christ is calling us to keep our side of the lawn mowed! He has provided this as a way out of the sin struggles that so easily entangle us. We get to work them out through an honest and humble heart check of our daily actions.

Normally when we are disturbed it's because we find somebody or some situation in our lives unacceptable. We can choose to blame others for our problems or use other people's problems as an excuse to misbehave. This robs us of our peace. Instead, we must choose to focus on our own yard, admitting when we are wrong and quickly taking ownership for our actions is the key to healthy daily heart checks.

Who or what have you blamed in the past for your mistakes?

_____

_____

_____

Have there been instances since starting this journey to a
healthy MANdentity when you have been wrong but didn't realize it until later? If so, what were they? _____

_____

_____

_____

This is one of my favorite passages of scripture:

And it came to pass, when David and his men were come to Ziklag
on the third day, that the Amalekites had invaded the south, and
Ziklag, and smitten Ziklag, and burned it with fire; And had taken
the women captives, that were therein: they slew not any, either
great or small, but carried them away, and went on their way. So
David and his men came to the city, and, behold, it was burned
with fire; and their wives, and their sons, and their daughters, were
taken captives. Then David and the people that were with him
lifted up their voice and wept, until they had no more power to
weep. And David's two wives were taken captives, Ahinoam the
Jezreelitess, and Abigail the wife of Nabal the Carmelite. And David was greatly distressed; for the people spoke of stoning him, because the soul of all the people was grieved, every man for his sons
and for his daughters: but David encouraged himself in the Lord
his God. (1 Samuel 30:1-6 KJV)

David had developed the keen ability to encourage himself based on what he knew to be true about God. This is a gift that every MANdentity man must take possession of. God has given the believer the holy spirit within to anchor us in times of trouble. Jesus Christ is the Messiah, the Savior of the world and His Word is for our lives.

Place yourself in David's shoes. He and his men were no doubt full of pride after a successful war campaign. They likely were eager to share their spoils with their families. David and his men were feeling good as they made the ride back to camp. As they approached and saw the smoke billowing from the camp, they quickly realize in their absence, in their quest for greatness, their very home had been destroyed and everything they had fought for was taken from them. Many of us have found ourselves right where David was and many of us are standing in David's shoes at this very moment. I envision David slowly dismounting his horse, looking around in disbelief, tears filling his eyes as the sounds of wailing men wanting to kill him fill his ears. What is David to do? He's lost everything trying to gain everything he thought he needed. In this anguish David turned to God. While the others were blaming him because of the pain of their souls, while his mistake of not leaving men to protect the women and children was ever apparent, David chooses to look to God. The strength of a man's identity is framed on him choosing God in hard times. When we choose God it's much easier to face our mistakes, make them right, and work to improve on our future endeavors. It's time for each of us to start taking responsibility for our choices and turning to God with the wrong choices we make.

What does quickly admitting you were wrong mean to you?

_____

_____

_____

> "For a righteous man may fall seven times and rise again, But the wicked shall fall by calamity." (Proverbs 24:16 NKJV)

It's easy to fall into the trap of only focusing on the negative things in our lives. We must be balanced and acknowledge our successes as well. Solomon teaches us that one of the differences between a wicked man and a righteous man is whether or not the man learns from his mistakes so as not to repeat them.

Have there been situations in your journey in which you felt uncomfortable about acknowledging something you had done right or well? Describe._____

_____

_____

Do you have any fears of success? Explain why or what has brought this on? _____

_____

_____

In your own words share why God wants you to be successful.

_____

_____

_____

MANdentity men prioritize the things we do in our lives. MANdentity is about transforming our daily thoughts, behaviors and overall choices to make them align with God's Word. This is how we walk out our faith and live a life in tune with the Spirit of God. Over the next seven days choose God by setting aside time in a quiet space to pray and answer the following questions one day at a time. I suggest doing your heart check before bed or opposite of when you read your Bible."

DAILY HEART CHECK

DAY 1

For each of the questions below, if you answer yes, please give a brief description.

Did you revert back to your old way of thinking or behaving today?

_____

_____

_____

Did you harm anyone today?

_____

_____

_____

Do you owe anyone an apology? (Check with your mentor before making any amends.)

_____

_____

_____

HEART CHECK

Did you allow yourself to become obsessed about anything?

_____

_____

_____

What did you do to be of service to others today? (For example, "I smiled at _____. I was kind to _____.)

_____

_____

_____

What have you done today about which you feel positive?

_____

_____

_____

What are you grateful for (list people, places, or things)?

_____

_____

_____

Thank God for the good and not so good from today.

DAY 2

For each of the questions below, if you answer yes, please give a brief description.

Did you revert back to your old way of thinking or behaving today?

_____

_____

_____

Did you harm anyone today?

_____

_____

_____

Do you owe anyone an apology? (Check with your mentor before making any amends.)

_____

_____

_____

_____

HEART CHECK

Did you allow yourself to become obsessed about anything?

_____

_____

_____

What did you do to be of service to others today? (For example, "I smiled at _____. I was kind to _____.)

_____

_____

_____

What have you done today about which you feel positive?

_____

_____

_____

What are you grateful for (list people, places, or things)?

_____

_____

_____

Thank God for the good and not so good from today.

DAY 3

For each of the questions below, if you answer yes, please give a brief description.

Did you revert back to your old way of thinking or behaving today?

_____

_____

_____

Did you harm anyone today?

_____

_____

_____

Do you owe anyone an apology? (Check with your mentor before making any amends.)

_____

_____

_____

_____

Did you allow yourself to become obsessed about anything?

_____

_____

_____

What did you do to be of service to others today? (For example, "I smiled at _____. I was kind to _____.)

_____

_____

_____

What have you done today about which you feel positive?

_____

_____

_____

What are you grateful for (list people, places, or things)?

_____

_____

_____

Thank God for the good and not so good from today.

DAY 4

For each of the questions below, if you answer yes, please give a brief description.

Did you revert back to your old way of thinking or behaving today?

_____

_____

_____

Did you harm anyone today?

_____

_____

_____

Do you owe anyone an apology? (Check with your mentor before making any amends.)

_____

_____

_____

_____

Did you allow yourself to become obsessed about anything?

_____

_____

_____

What did you do to be of service to others today? (For example, "I smiled at _____. I was kind to _____.)

_____

_____

_____

What have you done today about which you feel positive?

_____

_____

_____

What are you grateful for (list people, places, or things)?

_____

_____

_____

Thank God for the good and not so good from today.

DAY 5

For each of the questions below, if you answer yes, please give a brief description.

Did you revert back to your old way of thinking or behaving today?

_____

_____

_____

Did you harm anyone today?

_____

_____

_____

Do you owe anyone an apology? (Check with your mentor before making any amends.)

_____

_____

_____

_____

Did you allow yourself to become obsessed about anything?

_____

_____

_____

What did you do to be of service to others today? (For example, "I smiled at _____. I was kind to _____.)

_____

_____

_____

What have you done today about which you feel positive?

_____

_____

_____

What are you grateful for (list people, places, or things)?

_____

_____

_____

Thank God for the good and not so good from today.

DAY 6

For each of the questions below, if you answer yes, please give a brief description.

Did you revert back to your old way of thinking or behaving today?

_____

_____

_____

Did you harm anyone today?

_____

_____

_____

Do you owe anyone an apology? (Check with your mentor before making any amends.)

_____

_____

_____

_____

HEART CHECK

Did you allow yourself to become obsessed about anything?

_____

_____

_____

What did you do to be of service to others today? (For example, "I smiled at _____. I was kind to _____.)

_____

_____

_____

What have you done today about which you feel positive?

_____

_____

_____

What are you grateful for (list people, places, or things)?

_____

_____

_____

Thank God for the good and not so good from today.

DAY 7

For each of the questions below, if you answer yes, please give a brief description.

Did you revert back to your old way of thinking or behaving today?

_____

_____

_____

Did you harm anyone today?

_____

_____

_____

Do you owe anyone an apology? (Check with your mentor before making any amends.)

_____

_____

_____

_____

Did you allow yourself to become obsessed about anything?

_____

_____

_____

What did you do to be of service to others today? (For example, "I smiled at _____. I was kind to _____.)

_____

_____

_____

What have you done today about which you feel positive?

_____

_____

_____

What are you grateful for (list people, places, or things)?

_____

_____

_____

Thank God for the good and not so good from today.

This book is meant to teach you to live along biblical principles that both heal and guide. MANdentity is a lifelong journey of learning, loving and leading. We each embark on this journey one day at a time.

> Therefore I tell you, do not worry about your life, what you will eat or drink; or about your body, what you will wear. Is not life more than food, and the body more than clothes? Look at the birds of the air; they do not sow or reap or store away in barns, and yet your heavenly Father feeds them. Are you not much more valuable than they? Can any one of you by worrying add a single hour to your life? "And why do you worry about clothes? See how the flowers of the field grow. They do not labor or spin. Yet I tell you that not even Solomon in all his splendor was dressed like one of these. If that is how God clothes the grass of the field, which is here today and tomorrow is thrown into the fire, will he not much more clothe you—you of little faith? So do not worry, saying, 'What shall we eat?' or 'What shall we drink?' or 'What shall we wear?' For the pagans run after all these things, and your heavenly Father knows that you need them. But seek first his kingdom and his righteousness, and all these things will be given to you as well. Therefore do not worry about tomorrow, for tomorrow will worry about itself. Each day has enough trouble of its own. (Matthew 6:25-34)

It's important that we learn not to look too far ahead or get caught gazing in our past without a specific purpose for healing. We must not allow our enemy to convince us to focus our minds on the wreckage of the future or the disappointments of the past. Daily heart checks help focus our minds and hearts on today. God is with us in the present. This is another gift He provides. I encourage you to continue meeting with God each day and to set aside time to self-reflect. MANdentity men use this tool to become grounded with a deep and realistic sense of self. We learn to understand who we are in order to deeply impact those around us.

———

So then each of us will give an account of himself to God.
(Romans 14:12)

11
MEETING WITH JESUS

Stepping onto an airplane for the first time at twenty-two years old my heart was full of adventure. It was electrifying. I must admit taking off for the first time on that plane was not pleasant. And if it had not been for a sweet friend with a beautiful voice and warm smile singing hymns in my ear, I might have had a panic attack. The flight went well with almost no turbulence. The landing in San Francisco was another story. The runway ends on a cliff near the water. As we began to descend, it looked like the plane was headed for the water or the side of a small mountain. It was not the best runway for a first-time flyer!

As a kid I had dreamed of traveling to California and playing basketball in college. Then, as a new Christian, I was in California to play basketball. It was like watching a movie of my life in a dream.

Next door to my dorm was a fellow college student named James. He was something like I had never seen, literally. James was

Filipino, and I had never seen a Filipino person before. Growing up in rural west Tennessee was wonderful. There is nothing like small-town America in the Deep South, but in some areas there is a lack of diversity. My only experience as a young person with people of other ethnicities was watching sports, TV/movies, and working in the tobacco field with a Mexican named Federico.

James was very particular about how he dressed and especially about how his ties were tied. Many mornings he took the time to teach me how to tie my tie. One of the requirements was to always wear a shirt with a properly tied tie. If it was poorly tied, you would get demerits. James taught me how to tie a tie in multiple ways, how to iron my clothes with starch, how to share the Gospel, how to court a lady, and how to meet with Jesus each day.

Our friendship began with James knocking on my door in the mornings with a cup of coffee for me. He offered me help in so many different ways and then one day he asked me if he could share with me what he read in the Bible that morning. I accepted and listened for a few minutes to him talk about what God had showed him in the Bible that morning. Then one morning he showed up in my dorm room holding a notebook. James began to share with me an outline of how he met with Jesus each day. He would write down the passage of Scripture that he read along with the date at the top, a brief summary of what he read and then a quote from the Scripture at the bottom of the page. I was impressed, but he was not trying to impress me; he wanted to invest in me. The very next morning he showed up with a notebook for me and said, "You start meeting with Jesus and then we can share with each other what we got." I was reading the Bible daily, but there was not the intentionality that James was teaching me. It was more like something I did for God instead of an experience I had with God.

Every day for the next few months James and I shared with each other what we had read and what God had taught us through that reading. It was exhilarating for me. Each morning I could not wait to get up to read my Bible and write in my notebook. And sharing what I learned with James and listening to the word he got became the favorite part of my day. Something changed inside of me over that time. There was a thirst for an intimacy with Jesus that I had never experienced before. I had gone to Church religiously since my salvation, listen to Christian music, attended Sunday school, prayed, and read my Bible. All of those are important to spiritual health and add value to the Christian life. But for me those things were like putting on flip flops, a tank top, swimming trunks, and grabbing a float and merely standing next to the pool, never abiding in all the refreshing and reviving sensations the pool has to offer. I was missing the joy of experiencing the presence of God in an intentional and reflective way. My hope is that this chapter will teach you how to usher in the presence of God in your life as well.

MEETING WITH JESUS

MANdentity men connect with Jesus through prayer, Bible reading and scripture memory.

John 14:6 "Jesus said to him, "I am the way, and the truth, and the life. No one comes to the Father except through me."

Christianity is not about what we cannot do. It's not about the do nots. It's not a legal relationship. It's a love relationship. If you love someone, then you spend time with them. Not just any old time rushing here or there but quality heartfelt time. Throughout the Gospels Jesus is getting away from everything and everyone to be alone with the Father. It was an intentional act of love on Jesus's part, just as King David wrote:

> Oh, how I love Your law! It is my meditation all the day. You, through Your commandments, make me wiser than my enemies; For they are ever with me. I have more understanding than all my teachers, For Your testimonies are my meditation. I understand more than the ancients, Because I keep Your precepts. I have restrained my feet from every evil way, That I may keep Your word. I have not departed from Your judgments, For You Yourself have taught me. How sweet are Your words to my taste, Sweeter than honey to my mouth! Through Your precepts I get understanding; Therefore, I hate every false way. (Psalms 119:97-104 NKJV)

Jesus loves our Father in heaven and when on earth He desired to spend time with Him, so He made time to be with Him a priority. We have to do the same thing if we want to develop a deep devotion for Jesus and maintain a healthy way of life. There are some things that we don't do as Christians anymore, but the things we choose not to do because of our faith are not the foundation of Christianity. The foundation of a personal Christian faith is seeking a loving relationship with Jesus. In order to have a close relationship with Jesus, a consistent practice of silence and solitude with Him, reading and studying His word is non-negotiable. My former pastor, David Landrith, who went to be with Jesus, used to say, "A quiet time with Jesus is the 101 of Christianity. It's where everything starts."

I was twenty-three years old the first time someone sat me down and taught me how to have an effective time with Jesus. Three years after my conversion my Christian brother James finally took the time to share this powerful and life-changing tool. I have never been the same since and neither will you when you practice the following each day.

1. Find a quiet place early in the morning.

Where is a quiet place in your current living situation?

_____

_____

What time will you need to get up to have no distractions?

_____

_____

"O Lord; in the morning will I direct my prayer unto Thee and will look up." (Psalms 5:3 KJV)

2.   **Take a deep breath and focus your thoughts on God.** Try sitting in silence allowing your thoughts to bounce from thought to thought until they settle into a place of quiet anticipation. Then ask God to search your heart, to know you, to test you and to find the sin in your heart and to lead you to the way everlasting. Invite the holy spirit to fill you, to speak to you, and to guide your thoughts. Tell God you are ready to listen.

Is there something that is preventing you from silently listening to God? Is there something that keeps popping up that's preventing you from focusing on God?

_____

_____

_____

If so, using the table in Finding the Pain, chapter 5, write whatever is preventing you from listening to God in the first column.

Then, in the next column write the things you did in your past that were disturbing your peace. What do you need to accept and turn over to God? _____

_____

_____

_____

"Let the words of my mouth and the meditation of my heart be acceptable in your sight, O LORD, my rock and my redeemer." (Psalms 19:14 ESV)

3. **Get into the Word of God or read the Bible.** My friend and pastor, Robby Gallaty, often says, "When you get into the Word, the Word gets into you."

What has your experience with the Bible been like up to this point?

_____

_____

_____

Why is daily Bible reading important for your continued growth and healing? _____

_____

_____

_____

"All scripture is given by inspiration of God, and is profitable for doctrine, for reproof, for correction, for instruction in righteousness." (**2 Timothy 3:16 KJV**)

4. **Meditate on what you're reading throughout the day.** This reading time is for quality, not quantity.

Here are some ways you can practice meditating on God's Word throughout your day:

- Reread the same passage of Scripture throughout your day.
- Pray the truths of the Scripture into your life and over the lives of others.
- Memorize a passage or a portion of the Scriptures you read.
- Share what you learned from the Scriptures with someone else.

- Thank God throughout the day for the truth of the Scriptures you read.

"This Book of the Law shall not depart from your mouth, but you shall meditate on it day and night, so that you may be careful to do according to all that is written in it. For then you will make your way prosperous, and then you will have good success." (Joshua 1:8 NKJV)

5. Write down what God has given you through His Word.

Are you willing to write down how God has spoken to you through specific passages of scripture? _____

_____

_____

_____

If not, why? _____

_____

_____

_____

"Then the LORD said to Moses, "Write this for a memorial in the book and recount it in the hearing of Joshua."
(Exodus 17:14 NKJV)

6. Write down instructions, goals, and decisions revealed from your time with God.

What is your most important goal for today? _____

_____

_____

_____

_____

_____

What is your most important goal for this year? _____

_____

_____

_____

_____

_____

"But as for you, be strong and do not give up, for your work will be rewarded." (2 Chronicles 15:7)

7. **Pray, pour out your soul to God with reverence and honesty.** This is a time to express and share everything with Jesus. He already knows how you feel and desires to comfort you.

Use the lines below for your own personal prayer list. _____

_____

_____

_____

_____

Read the heartfelt prayer of David: "I am weary with my moaning; every night I flood my bed with tears; I drench my couch with my weeping" (Psalm 6:6 ESV).

Paul tells us that "Blessed be the God and Father of our Lord Jesus Christ, the Father of mercies and God of all comfort, [4] who comforts us in all our affliction, so that we may be able to comfort those who are in any affliction, with the comfort with which we ourselves are comforted by God" (2 Corinthians 1:3-4 ESV). Share all your burdens, fears and hope for change to God in prayer.

"Do not be anxious about anything, but in everything by prayer and supplication with thanksgiving let your requests be made known to God. 7 And the peace of God, which surpasses all understanding, will guard your hearts and your minds in Christ Jesus." (Philippians 4:6-7)

8. **Start practicing sharing what you read with others throughout your day.** We should be in the habit of exhorting and encouraging one another.

Is there a specific passage of scripture that has helped you during this season of life? If so, write why and how it has helped you.

_____

_____

_____

_____

_____

Do you have any family members that do not have a personal relationship with Jesus Christ? If so, please list their names and commit to praying for them. _____

_____

_____

_____

_____

_____

9. **Obey what God tells you in His word.** Adrian Rogers once said, "Our relationship with Jesus is built on revelation from His word and obedience to His word. We cannot have one without the other."

What passage of Scripture are you having trouble obeying right now? _____

_____

_____

_____

_____

Is there a passage of Scripture that you have trouble believing?

_____

_____

_____

_____

"If you love Me, keep My commandments."
(John 14:15 NKJV)

I remember hearing on ESPN that Kobe Bryant often shot over one thousand shots after games. His drive for NBA greatness made him one of the greatest players to ever play the game. The Christian life is not a game, and the stakes are immeasurable higher than any sport. This is about earthly hope and healing followed by an eternal life or death. Our part is to keep practicing our faith each day and that begins with a frequent quiet time with Jesus Christ.

For the next seven days practice the quiet time principles listed below:

- Find a quiet place early in the morning.
- Take a deep breath and focus your thoughts on God.
- Read the Bible.
- Write down what God has given you through His Word.

- Write down instructions, goals, and decisions revealed from your time with God.

- Meditate on what you're reading throughout the day.

- Pray.

- Practice sharing what you read with others throughout your day.

- Obey what God tells you in His Word.

I pray the same prayer that Paul prayed for the people of Ephesus over you:

> For this reason I bow my knees to the Father of our Lord Jesus Christ, from whom the whole family in heaven and earth is named, that He would grant you, according to the riches of His glory, to be strengthened with might through His Spirit in the inner man, that Christ may dwell in your hearts through faith; that you, being rooted and grounded in love, may be able to comprehend with all the saints what *is* the width and length and depth and height—to know the love of Christ which passes knowledge; that you may be filled with all the fullness of God. (Ephesians 3:14-19 NKJV)

12
HELPING OTHERS

My father owned a construction company before alcoholism took over his life. He could fix or operate any piece of equipment. His fingernails were always filled with grease and the knees of his jeans dirty. I was quite the opposite. I wore Michael Jordan shoes without a speck of dust and gel spiked my hair. Most of my days, before my dad's alcoholism and my mom's drug addiction, were spent at the pool, on the basketball court, or in my room playing video games. When I was a kid Dad worked hard so that I did not have too, but he failed to pass down much knowledge about fixing things.

After being released from the Salvation Army men's rehabilitation program at the age of twenty-five via a jail furlough, I received a job in the medical wheelchair industry. The job consisted of building, repairing, and adjusting power wheelchairs. All of which required basic knowledge of mechanical work—a skill I did not possess and had to work hard to learn. My days on the job were in a way like my dad's. I spent my time on my knees turning tools and getting dirty.

In my heart the opportunity to serve in full-time ministry had passed me by. I thought I had burned that bridge after running from the call God had on my life before my arrest. I ran right back to a life of alcohol and drugs. Now released, my wife and I started attending a local church on Sundays and gradually began to serve. A man named Henry was leading one of the ministries in which we served. Henry asked me if I would be willing to have lunch with him periodically. I agreed and we set a recurring time for lunch. He would drive to my work, pick me up in my dirty greasy attire, and take me to lunch.

Our conversations were not normal to me. He would ask me things like, "How's your heart? How's your marriage?" Every month he would show up at my work just to invest in me. Over time he began to stir in me a desire to help others as he was helping me. In the back of my mind I began to wonder if I could one day serve God full-time again.

A few weeks later another man, Mike, asked me if I had a mentor. I told him that I did, but we did not call each other. Mike laughed and said, "So the answer is no, you don't have a mentor!" He gave me his number and in his Michigan accent, "Call me on your way home from work tomorrow, Addeem." For the past ten years not a single week has gone by that we didn't text or call. Mike knows everything about me, and we've been through the MAN-dentity principles several times. My life is better today because of his investment in it. My life is better because Mike answers the phone when I call. I wanted to start replicating for others what Mike and Henry did and do for me. "Iron sharpens iron, and one man sharpens another" (Proverbs 27:17). A few years later I met a young man in the ministry at a luncheon for local youth pastors in our county.

We started meeting regularly for lunch. I started out asking him the same questions Mike and Henry asked me. Over the years I've added more questions to my tool pouch of investing in others. There is no doubt in my mind that emotional and spiritual growth expands as we help others. At many points in my journey helping others is the only thing I could do to get through a difficult situation. It has become a daily practice for me. I used to think that I did not know enough about the Bible or that I did not have enough time living clean and close to Jesus to help someone else. We will never know it all or have it all figured out. Often, we grow the most by practicing with humility what we learn as we serve other people. Over time my efforts to help others began to help me. Helping others taught me my weaknesses and my strengths. Journeying with another man on his MANdentity journey took me farther and closer to Jesus than I had ever been before. It will do the same for you!

HELPING OTHERS

MANdentity men serve their family, their church and their community.

"For you were called to freedom, brothers. Only do not use your freedom as an opportunity for the flesh, but through love serve one another. For the whole law is fulfilled in one word: "You shall love your neighbor as yourself." (Galatians 5:13-14 ESV)

The apostle Luke recounts a time when Jesus healed a leper:

> While he was in one of the cities, there came a man full of leprosy. And when he saw Jesus, he fell on his face and begged him, "Lord, if you will, you can make me clean." And Jesus stretched out his hand and touched him, saying, "I will; be clean." And immediately the leprosy left him. (Luke 5:12-13 ESV)

A man his wife, their ten-year-old son and four-year-old daughter purchased some land, and the man was building a small house on it. One day he noticed a small white spot on his left hand between his thumb and pointer finger. The white spot became so soar that he decided not to work on the house that day. He thought the spot was due to over working his hand with a building tool. After a few days the spot did not go away and seemed to get worse. Him and his wife decide to go see a doctor for an examination. The doctor ran multiple tests and determined that the man would need to stay two weeks for more testing and at the end of those two weeks he would give a diagnosis. Two weeks pass and the white spot has spread all over the man's arm. The doctor walks into his room declaring that the man has leprosy. He tells the man that he must immediately go live outside the city. He is no longer allowed to touch or to even be near anyone and if someone happens to walk towards him, he must yell, "Unclean! Unclean!"

Realizing that his arm was the only part of his body infected so far, the man begs the doctor to allow him to go hug his wife, read to his daughter and wrestle with his son one last time only using his left hand. The doctor shakes his head sharing that the man would be risking them getting the infection by going near them at all. Over the next twenty years the man's body slowly falls apart. He lost fingers, ears and almost all feeling. In most cases, Leprosy eventually causes your whole body to go numb. When someone is blind, they cannot see; when someone is deaf, they cannot hear; when someone has leprosy, they cannot feel. The infected parts of their body go numb and eventually lose all sensitivity.

For years the man has felt nothing. He's physically broken, spiritually hopeless and emotionally dead. He no longer wants his family to come see him because of the dire condition he's in. Then

Jesus approaches this man. "While he was in one of the cities, there came a man full of leprosy" (Luke 5:12). Can you visualize the man full of leprosy more clearly now? Physically broken, emotionally broken, literally numb with no one. All alone. "And when he saw Jesus, he fell on his face and begged him, 'Lord, if you will, you can make me clean.' And Jesus stretched out his hand and touched him." The word used for *touch* in the Greek is a much stronger word than the English translation of "touch." The Greek could literally be translated, Jesus took hold of him. Jesus embraces him before He is clean. Imagine how long it has been since someone touched him? Jesus was not just for loving others; Jesus is one who loves with others. To love is to be with a person in their struggles not to just be for them.

To love like Jesus, you must be transformed from the inside, not performing on the outside. All the work of the previous eleven chapters is not just for your healing. It's so that you can go help others heal. It's so you can go love others in the midst of their pain. We are to follow the model of Jesus and be with those around us. We are to be an example of love to the people in our lives as we continue to abide in the love of Jesus. Without genuine love for others are good deeds are simple moral actions with no heavenly impact. God is not hoping for spectacular deeds, he hoping to have a loving relationship with you that overflows into the people around you. Jesus desires that we love others as we love ourselves.

If I speak in the tongues of men and of angels, but have not love, I am a noisy gong or a clanging cymbal. 2 And if I have prophetic powers, and understand all mysteries and all knowledge, and if I have all faith, so as to remove mountains, but have not love, I am nothing. 3 If I give away all I have, and if I deliver up my body to be burned, but have not love, I gain nothing (1 Corinthians 13:1-3)

Our struggles had left us disconnected, often separated from the ones who loved us and from the ones we loved. We often lived in close proximity but still disconnected. My hope and prayer is that you would be completely transformed by the powerful Gospel of Jesus Christ and that you would be restored by the healing process of the previous eleven chapters. If you have not completed any of the questions or actions presented in the previous chapters, I beg you to do so right now.

We all have defining moments in our lives. Those moments we never will forget. I remember sitting in Pastor Joey's office as tears ran down my face on a Monday morning. My dad and his best friend, John, sat on a bench just large enough to fit the both of them across the room. A year earlier my dad gave his life to Jesus Christ thanks to the help of John. He and his friends began to pray for me in the basement of John's house. After living in my car for a year and not speaking to my dad, I decided to try and find him. I walked into that basement on a Sunday afternoon just as my dad and his friends had returned from Church. And now I sat in their pastor's office twenty years old with no purpose or plan for my life. The tears were prompted simply by him asking me, "Why are you here?"

"I feel like I have two big bulldozers on my shoulders. I don't know what to do with my life," I replied. After a few seconds of silence that felt like eternity, I realized Pastor Joey was waiting for me to say more. I squirmed in my seat a little and said, "You know, it feels like there's been a video camera over my shoulder. Like someone is watching me, been there my entire life."

Pastor Joey leaned forward and began to explain through Scripture who Jesus Christ is and how He gave His life for me. As he explained the son of God to me the tears fell, and on that day I was transformed. I've never been the same. Since then I've been to jail, lost jobs, had people die, failed in emotionally supporting my wife at times, and on and on, but I was changed on that day. It was a spiritual awakening of sorts. There was no burning bush, bright light, or verbal words from heaven, but it was like scales fell off my soul and I could see an entirely new world in front of me. It was as if the fog of my life was lifted, and I could think clearly now.

MANdentity men should be able to relate to the leper in the story in Luke because our sin struggles in many ways outcasted us. This is very important because without an encounter with Jesus Christ, you will not possess the power and prompting of the Holy Spirit necessary to impact the lives of others for eternity. If you have never agreed with God about your sin and confessed it to

Christ, please do so now. If you have never truly repented of your sins and asked God to save your soul through your belief in Jesus Christ, please do so now. If you have never told God directly that you believe in His Son's death and resurrection alone for eternal salvation, please do so now. If you have not made a decision for Christ, I encourage to re-read chapter 2, Finding the Power. In addition, if you just made a decision for Jesus Christ, please contact your mentor, spiritual counselor, pastor and/or message me at theadamfrench.com. I promise you that we will be overjoyed and celebrate with your decision. Let's take a look at how far we have come since starting the MANdentity journey.

In what areas have you grown since starting the journey to MANdentity? _____

_____

_____

_____

_____

_____

_____

List some specific thought patterns or belief systems that have changed since coming to Christ and working through this book?

_____

_____

_____

_____

_____

What specific behaviors have changed since beginning the MAN-dentity process? _____

_____

_____

_____

_____

Share some relationships that have improved since beginning this journey? _____

_____

_____

_____

_____

Why have those relationships improved? Be as specific as possible.

_____

_____

_____

_____

In regard to your specific struggle, how has this study helped you
heal, overcome, and cope in healthy ways? _____

_____

_____

_____

Read the passage about Jesus healing the demon possessed man:

> [The disciples and Jesus] came to the other side of the sea, to the
> country of the Gerasenes. And when Jesus had stepped out of the
> boat, immediately there met Him out of the tombs a man with an
> unclean spirit. He lived among the tombs. And no one could bind
> him anymore, not even with a chain, for he had often been bound
> with shackles and chains, but he wrenched the chains apart, and he
> broke the shackles in pieces. No one had the strength to subdue
> him. Night and day among the tombs and on the mountains he was
> always crying out and cutting himself with stones. And when he
> saw Jesus from afar, he ran and fell down before Him. And crying
> out with a loud voice, he said, "What have you to do with me,

Jesus, Son of the Most High God? I adjure you by God, do not tor-
ment me." For He was saying to him, "Come out of the man, you
unclean spirit!" And Jesus asked him, "What is your name?" He
replied, "My name is Legion, for we are many." And he begged Him
earnestly not to send them out of the country. Now a great herd of
pigs was feeding there on the hillside, and they begged Him, saying,
"Send us to the pigs; let us enter them." So He gave them permis-
sion. And the unclean spirits came out and entered the pigs; and
the herd, numbering about two thousand, rushed down the steep
bank into the sea and drowned in the sea.

The herdsmen fled and told it in the city and in the country. And
people came to see what it was that had happened. And they came
to Jesus and saw the demon-possessed man, the one who had had
the legion, sitting there, clothed and in his right mind, and they
were afraid. And those who had seen it described to them what had
happened to the demon-possessed man and to the pigs. And they
began to beg Jesus to depart from their region. As He was getting
into the boat, the man who had been possessed with demons begged
Him that he might be with Him. And He did not permit him but
said to him, "Go home to your friends and tell them how much the
Lord has done for you, and how he has had mercy on you." And he
went away and began to proclaim in the Decapolis how much Jesus
had done for him, and everyone marveled. (Mark 5:1-20 ESV)

Just as Jesus told the demon-possessed man to go tell his
friends all that He had done for him, Jesus is telling us to do the
same. As MANdentity men we are supposed to carry the message of
Jesus Christ and the message of emotional and spiritual healing to
the world. In a sense, we keep what we have by giving it away. Jesus could have brought the man on the boat with the disciples.
There was plenty of room plus He knew Judas would eventually
betray Him! So why not take him? Jesus was giving this man the
very action that would continue the work He began in his heart.

Think of it this way, Jesus knew that a demonically possessed man who lived in a graveyard and inflicting physical harm on himself had many emotional scars. Jesus sent him back out to the world because humanity needs to hear his story. He also sent him back out to help others because Jesus knew that this man was still in need. His name was written in the Lamb's Book of Life and his eternal salvation in Jesus was secured, but he had a life in front of him that required emotional healing. As we help others we help ourselves. Helping others overcome their struggles is part of our continued healing. In fact, there will be times in your life in which your only defense against going back to old behaviors, old thinking, and your old struggle is to simple help someone else.

Why is it important for you to help others who struggle in the areas that you have struggled? _____

_____

_____

_____

_____

_____

We must remember to read this passage very carefully. Jesus says in verse nineteen that he should "tell them how much the LORD has done for you, and how He has had mercy on you." The MANdentity lifestyle is a lifestyle of attraction to Christ not promotion of ourselves. In terms of the Gospel we are commanded by Scripture to go and tell the world about Jesus. As Christ followers we should be sharing our faith with anyone and everyone that God allows to cross our path.

In what ways have you come across as arrogant or prideful when sharing your faith or victories with others in the past?

_____

_____

_____

_____

How can you practice humility while sharing your successes, victories, and your faith with others? _____

_____

_____

_____

_____

Is there anyone in your circle of influence that would benefit from
the MANdentity material? _____

_____

_____

_____

You may be wondering as this book comes to a close, "Am I a MANdentity man? Is there more for me to do?" Yes and no. Yes, every MANdentity man must continue to practice the principles outlined in this book to find continued healing and to develop healthier connections with others. No, there is not *more* for you to accomplish to become a MANdentity man in an outward sense. This book and the lifestyle of a MANdentity man is not about outward accomplishments. It's about inner wholeness, deep connections, and practicing the principles outlined in the book in all your affairs. As we continue to do the work, God restores, as He already has for many of you, and creates a mosaic of who we truly are. Each of us is a wonderful and magnificent picture of broken pieces brought together by the saving and healing power of Jesus Christ.

Today, I have accomplished much and I have much, but so do lots of men who are miserable and have no idea who they truly are. I'm not concerned with titles and outward accomplishments anymore. I most certainly have ambitions and goals, but more success isn't the point of a MANdentity man. My life today is far from perfect, and I have plenty of mistakes yet to be made. But I can say that I love myself. I know who I truly am, and I am at peace. I'm striving to live sacrificially with my wife. I'm with my kids every day, and I strive to help others to the best of my abilities. *More* for the MANdentity man is *more* of what makes him whole: more peace, more human connections, more honesty, more joy, more memories with the people you love, more help offered to others, and more of the *real* you living life to the best of your ability. You are a MANdentity man, and my challenge is for you to continue becoming one.

About the Author

Hunting and running through the woods of west Tennessee is a drastically different scene than selling drugs and rubbing shoulders with drug dealers in the inner city. This is the story of Adam French, a story of humble and healthy beginnings, a story of harsh and horrific interruption and a story wrapped in the life changing love of Christ. His Dad's journey of successful business owner to alcoholic coincides with his mother's struggle of a successful teacher to pill addict. Somewhere in the middle of their stories is a scared little boy, broken teenager and a wounded man. For the past 17yrs Adam has been on a journey of healing.

Adam draws from his counseling degree, bible college education, personal recovery, and pastoral experience to create an on ramp in his book, MANdentity, for men seeking healing in their marriages, addictions, traumas, broken relationships, and everyday struggles. MANdentity is designed for any man with any struggle to find healing. It's purposely written to be simple and direct, so that every man can heal by working through this book. All men have wounds. The MANdentity book intends to heal them.

Today, Adam travels sharing the redemptive story of Grace that Jesus brought to his life through his personal journey to MAN-dentity. He is a Bible communicator who encourages others to live out their faith. You will be challenged, motivated and encouraged by his teaching. If you feel led to have Adam come speak or share his story from a pulpit, classroom, conference, camp, school assembly, or business go to theadamfrench.com or @theadamfrench for booking opportunities.

Made in the USA
Middletown, DE
29 February 2024

50575207R00119